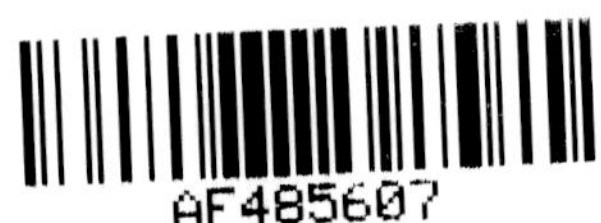

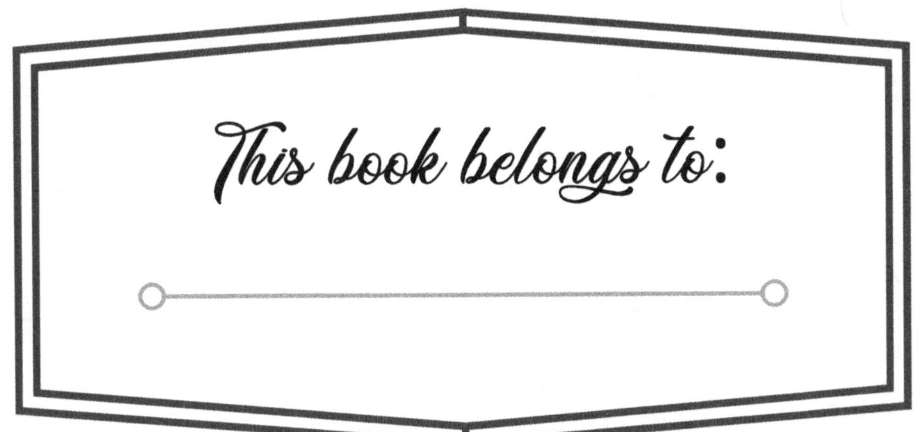

COLORFUL FLOWER DESIGNS

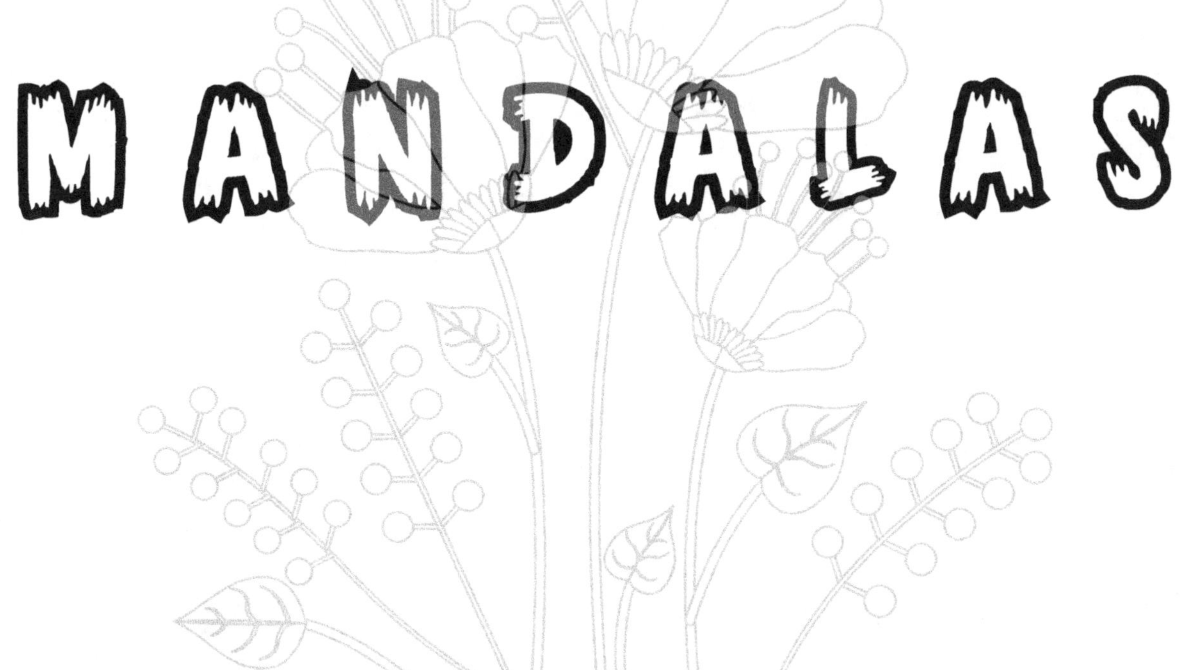

MANDALAS

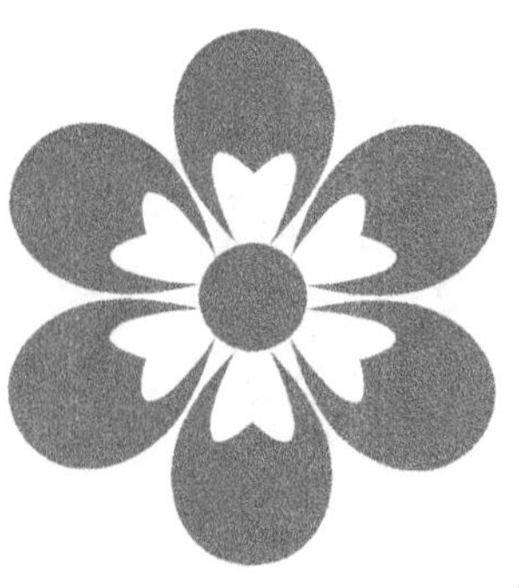

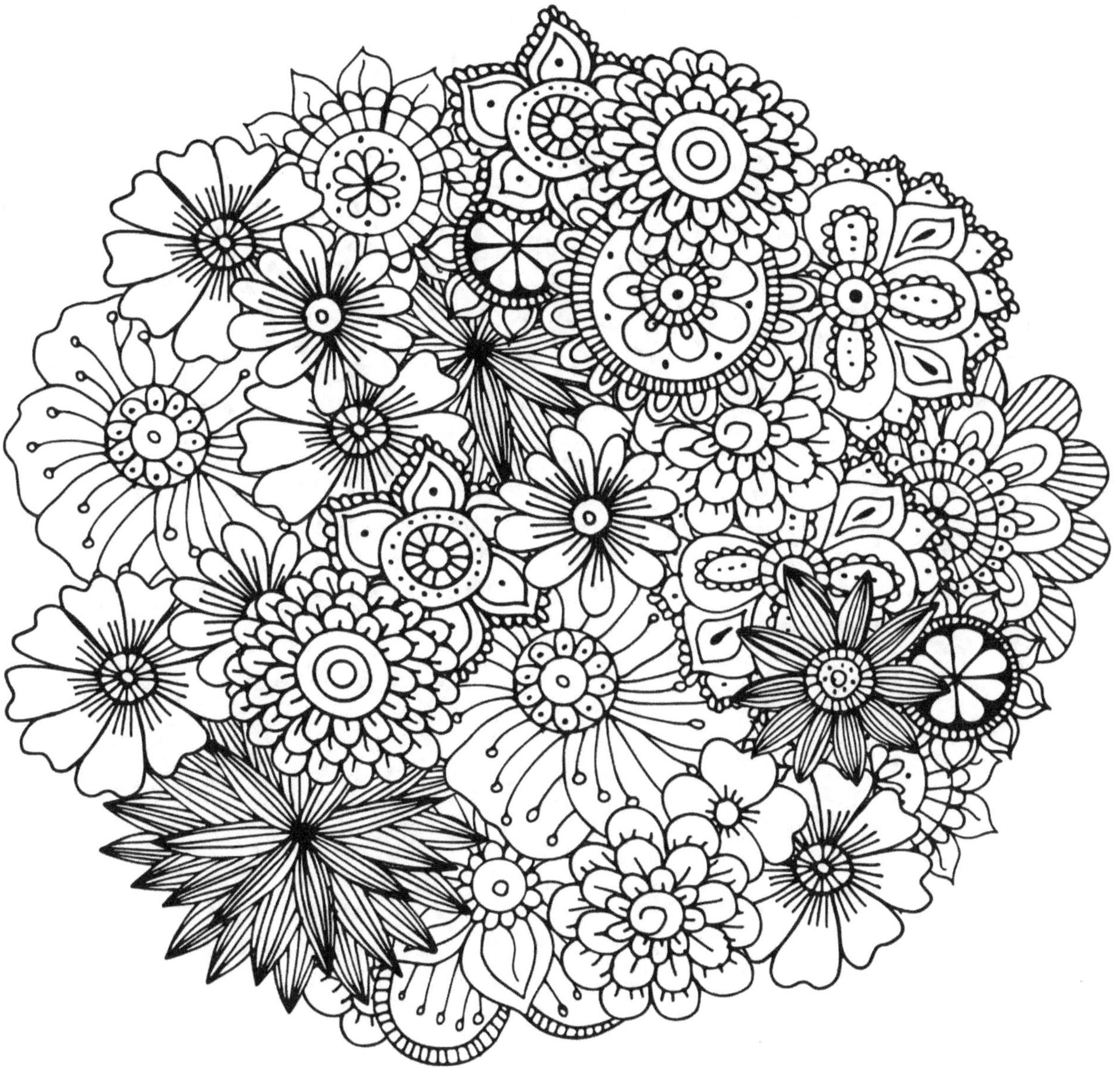

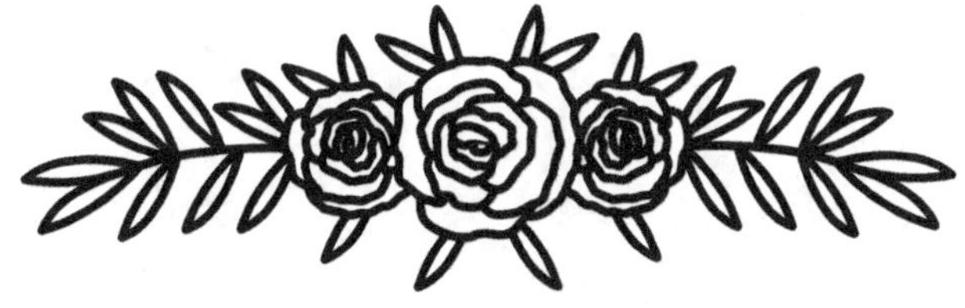

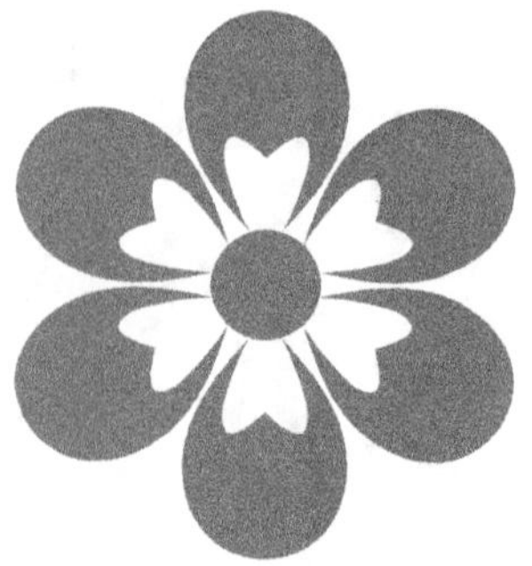

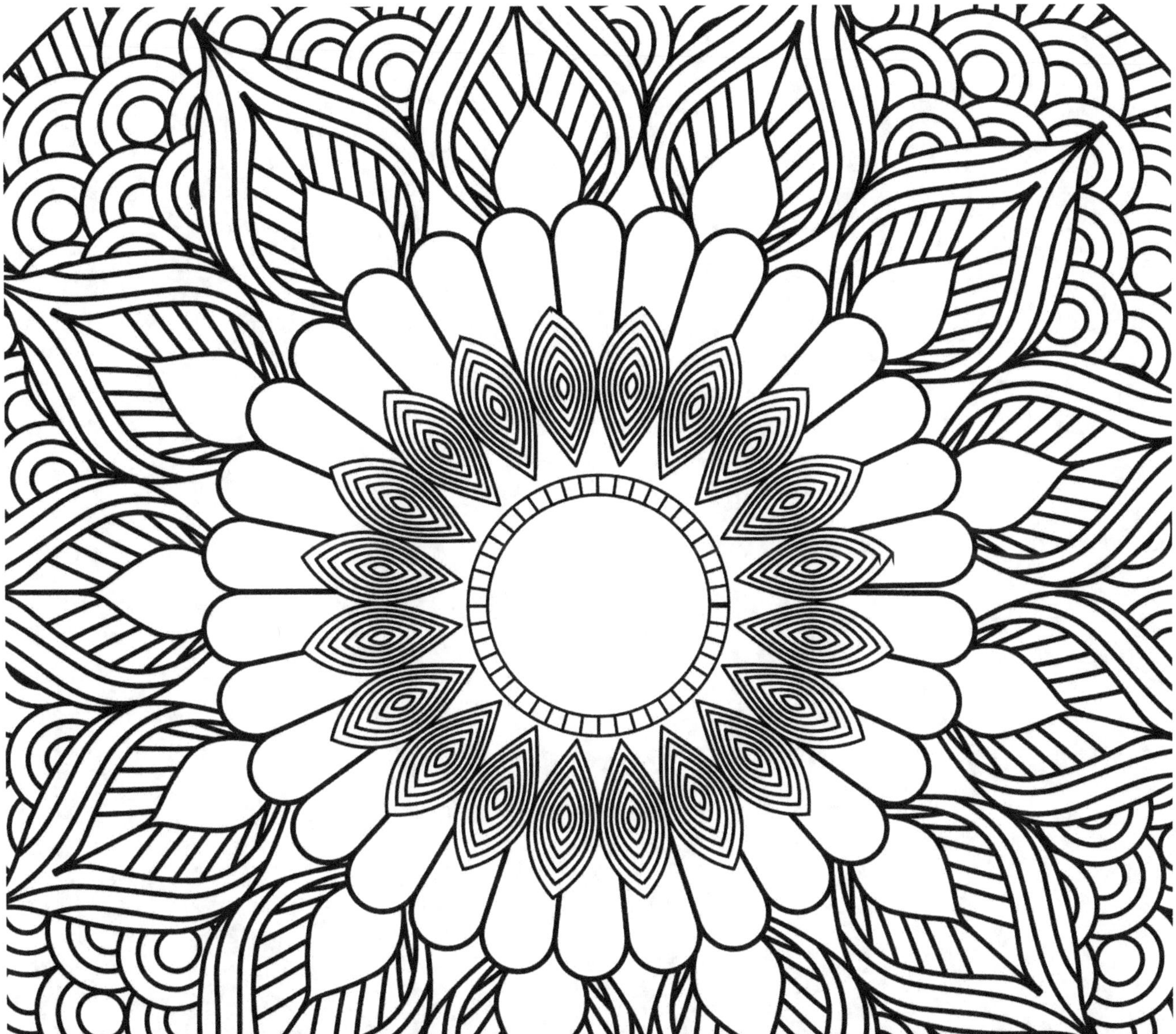

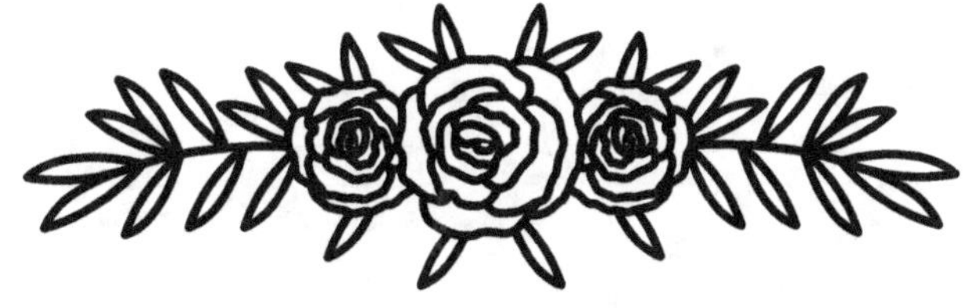

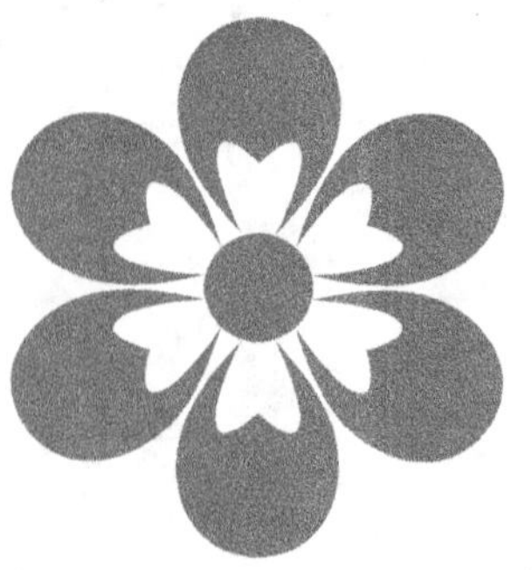

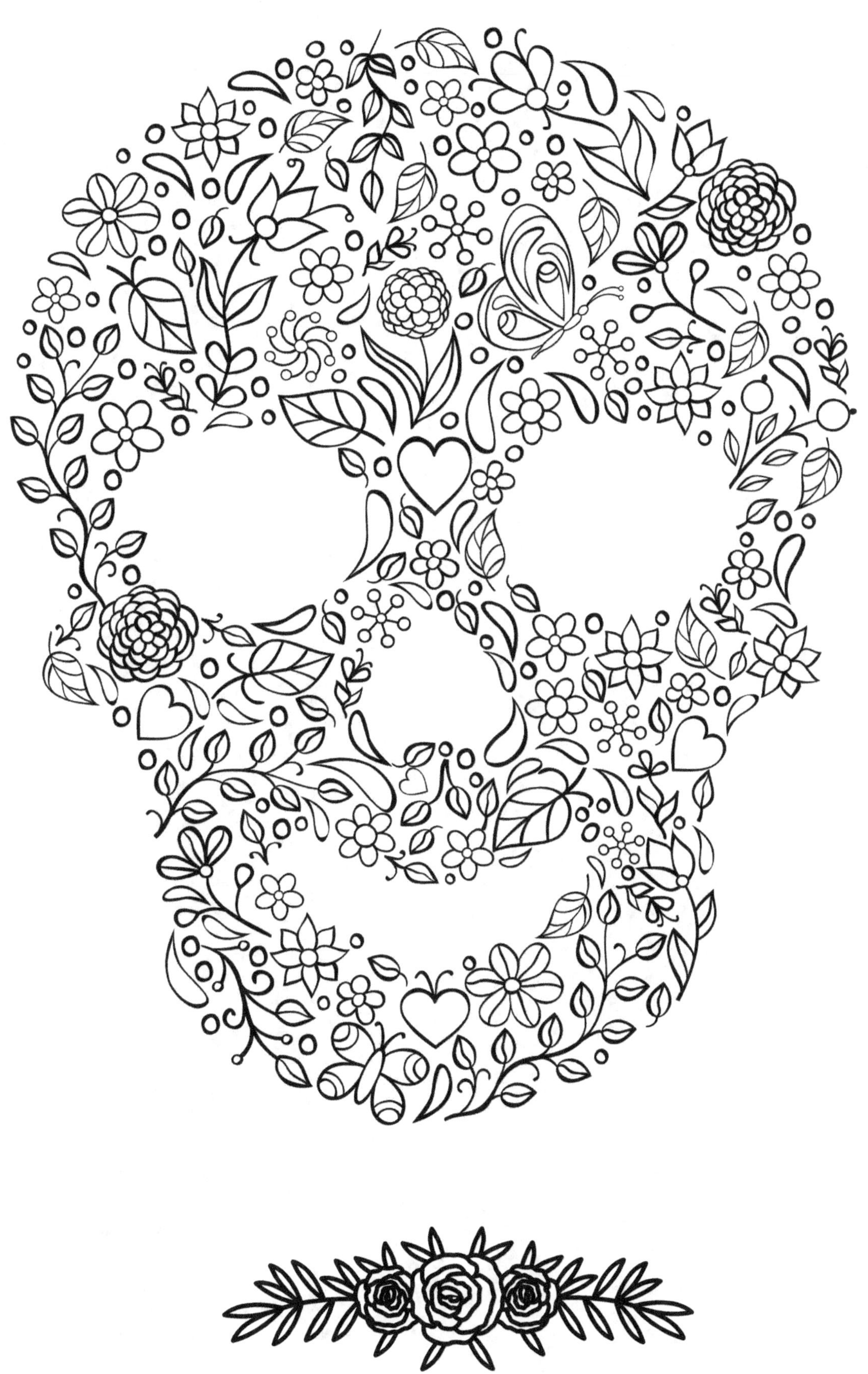

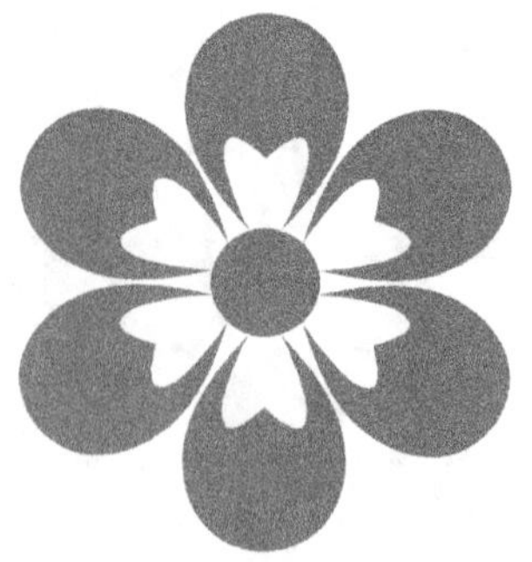

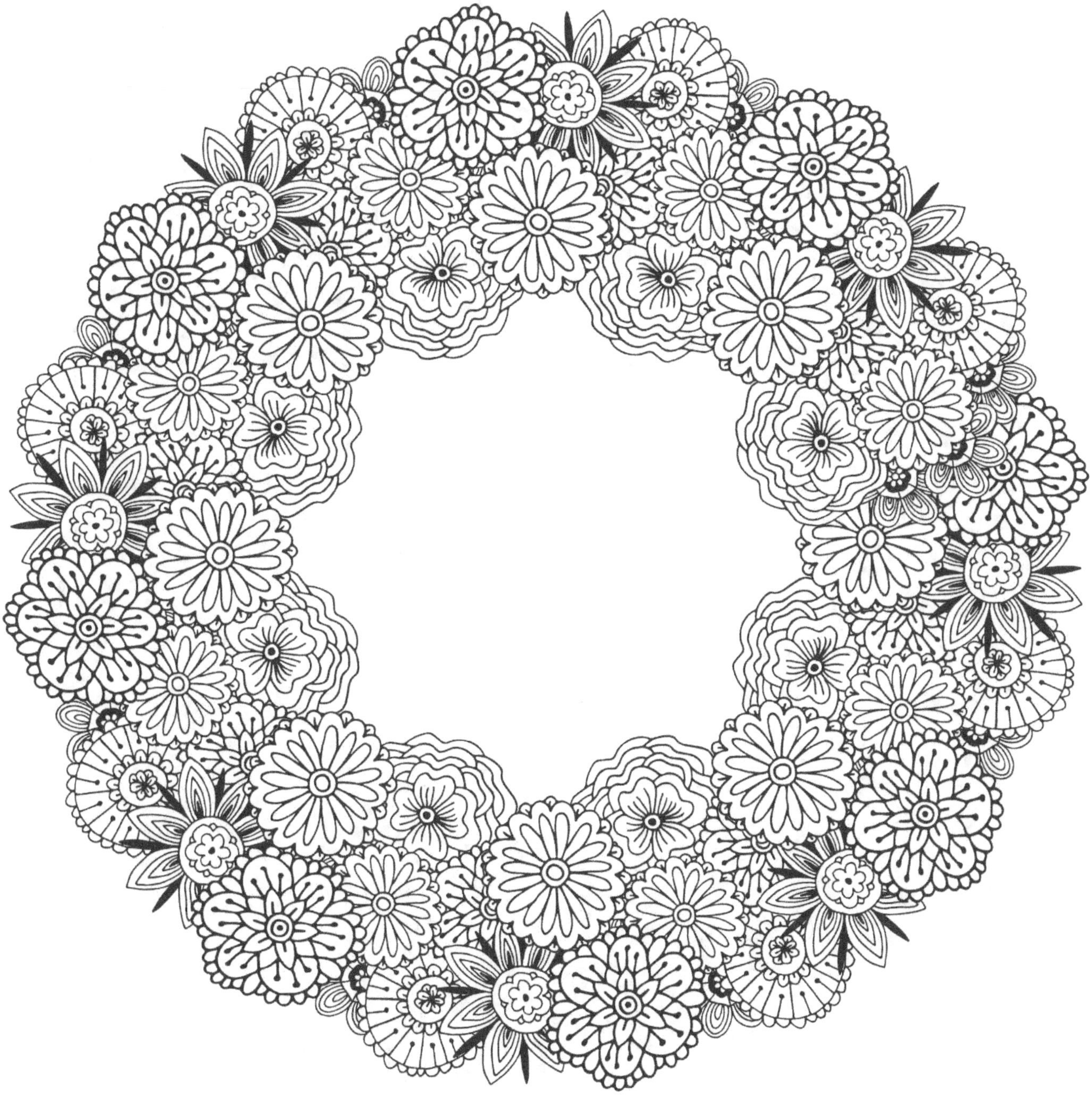

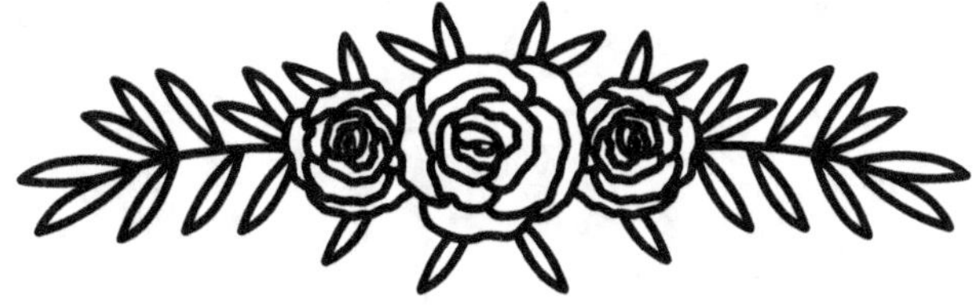

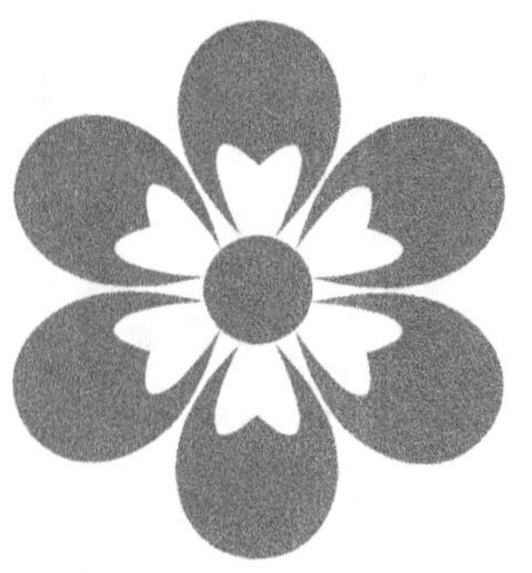

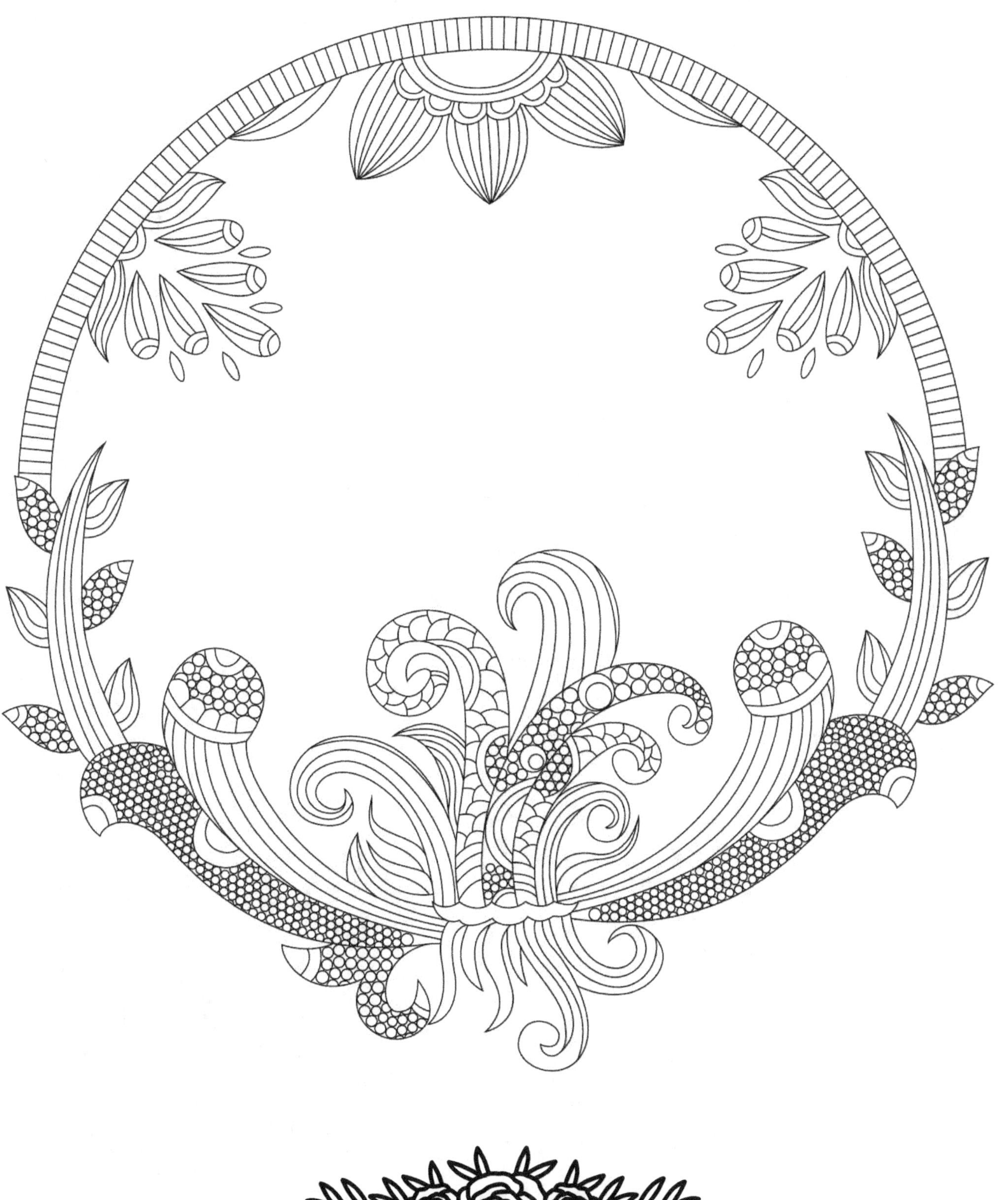

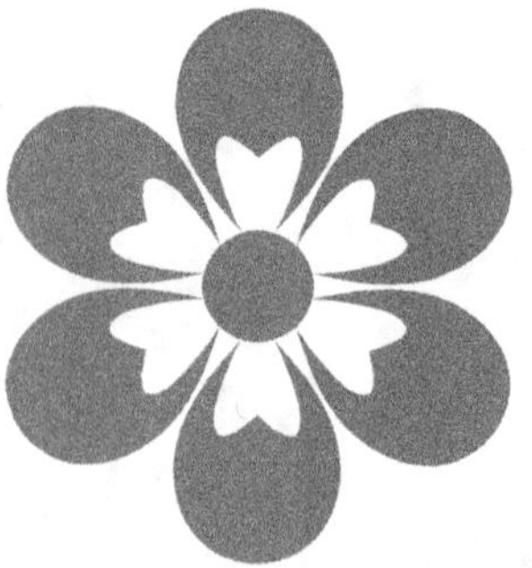

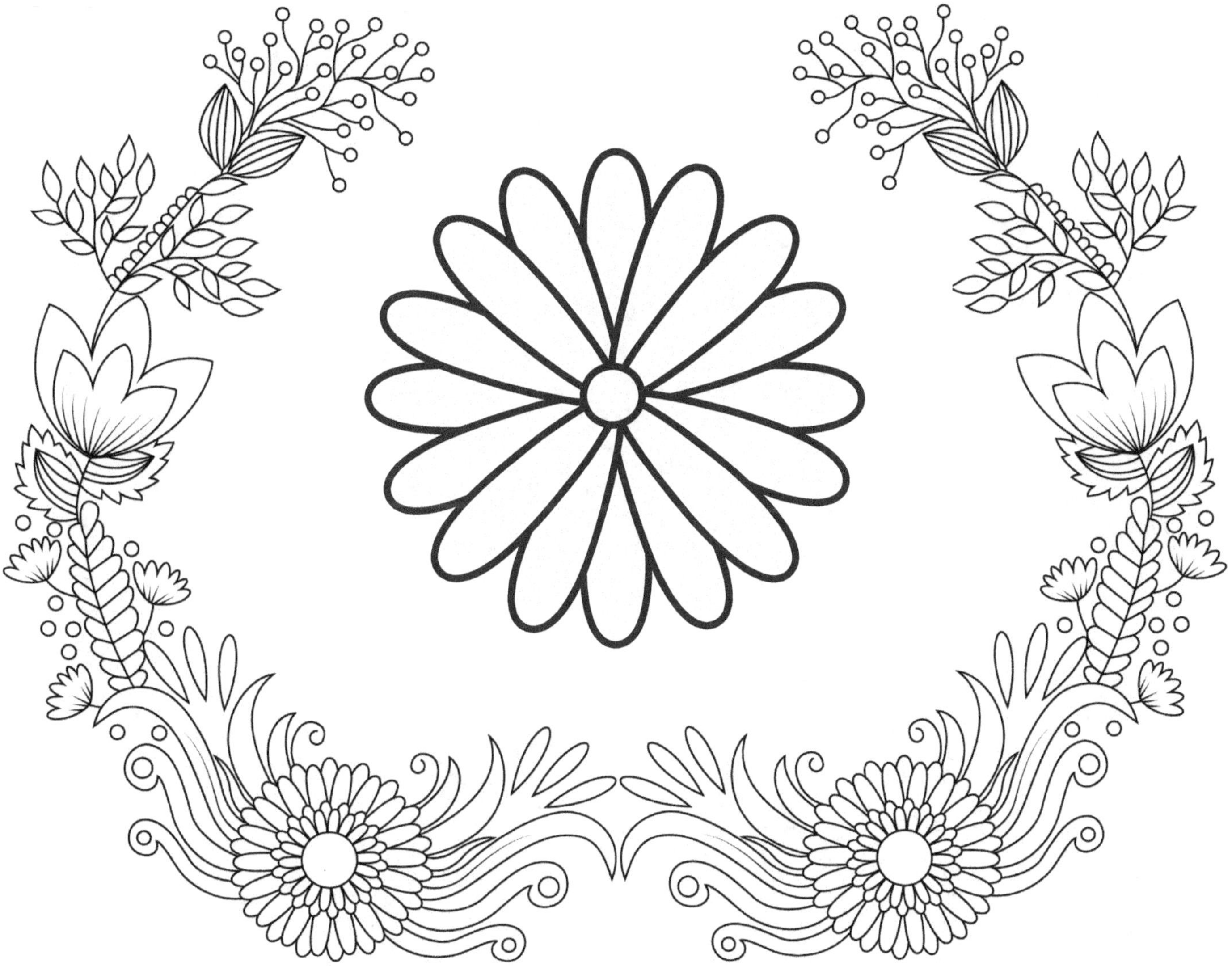

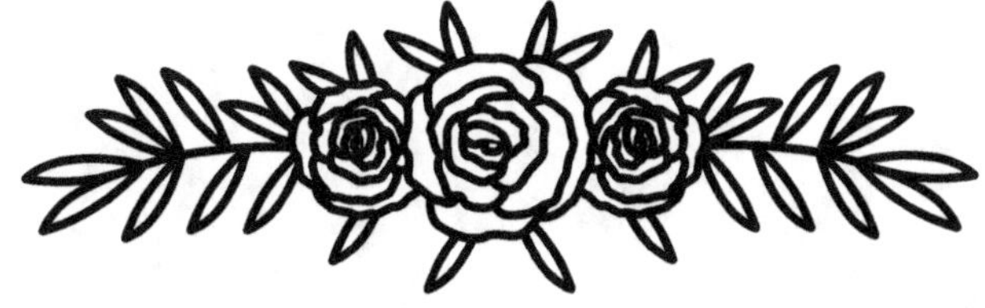

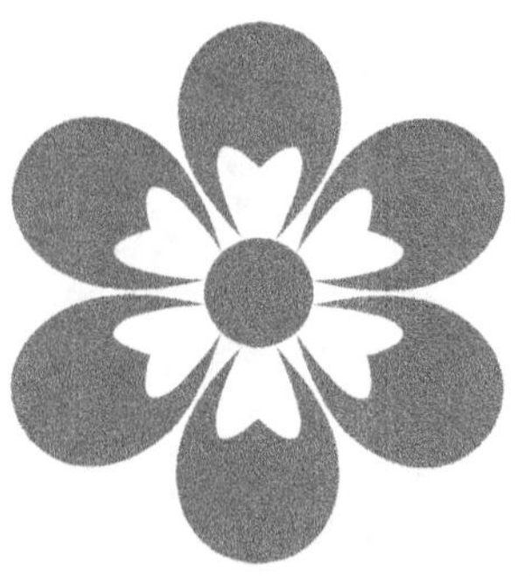

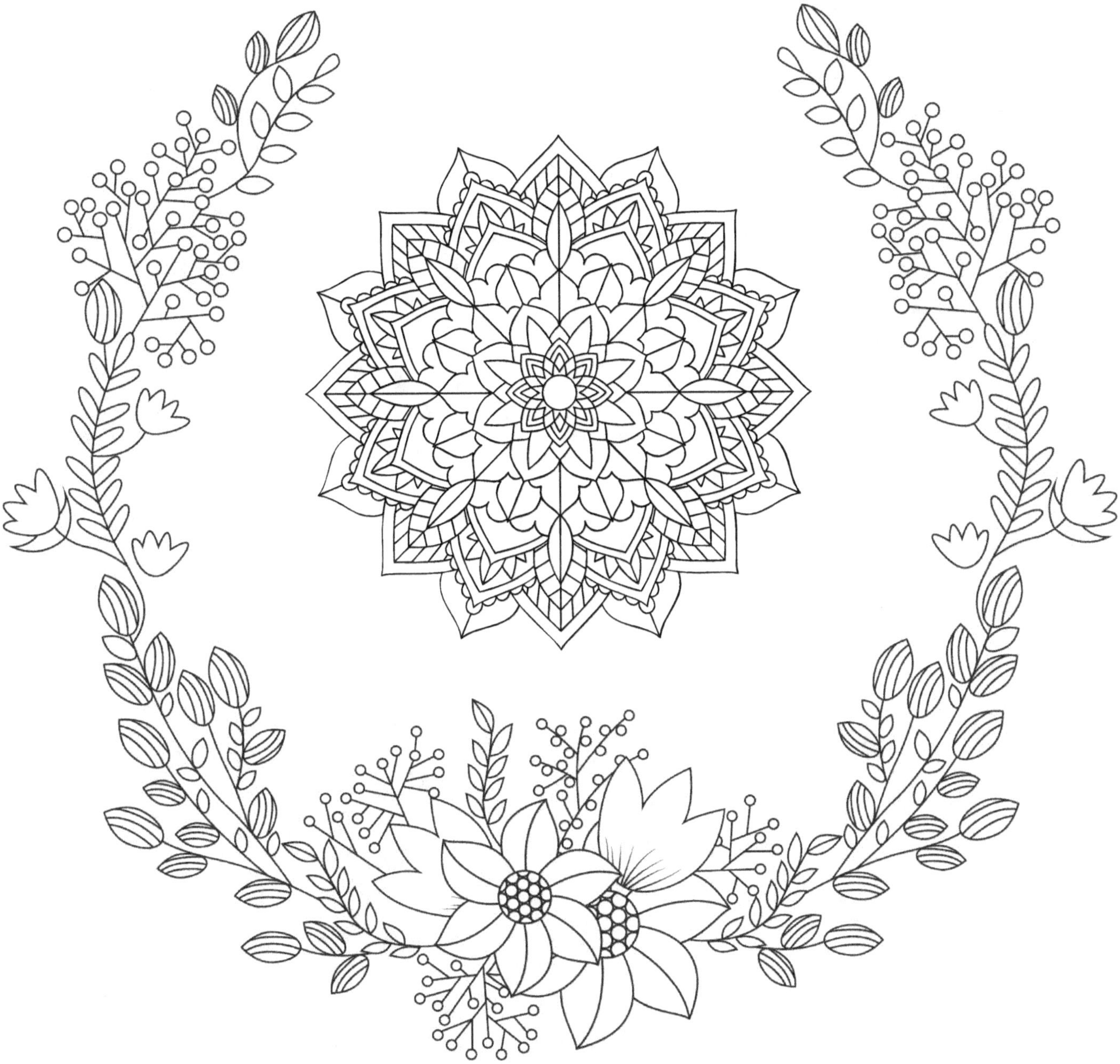

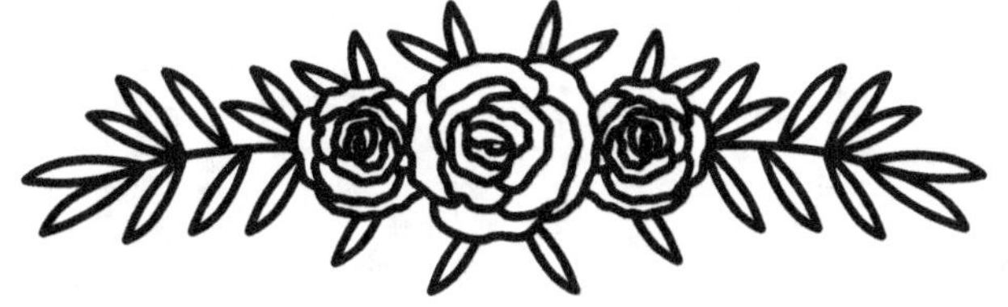

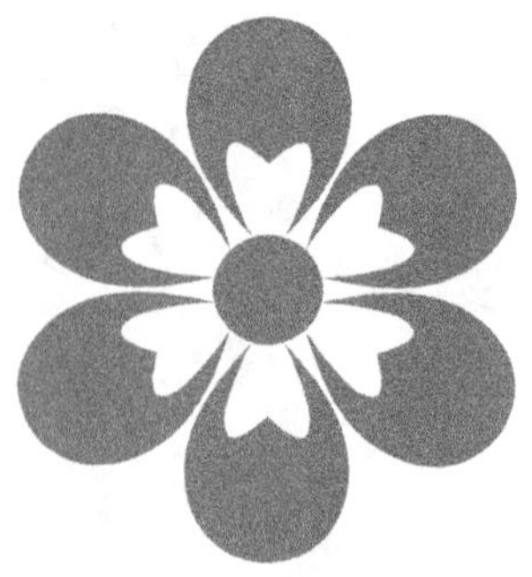

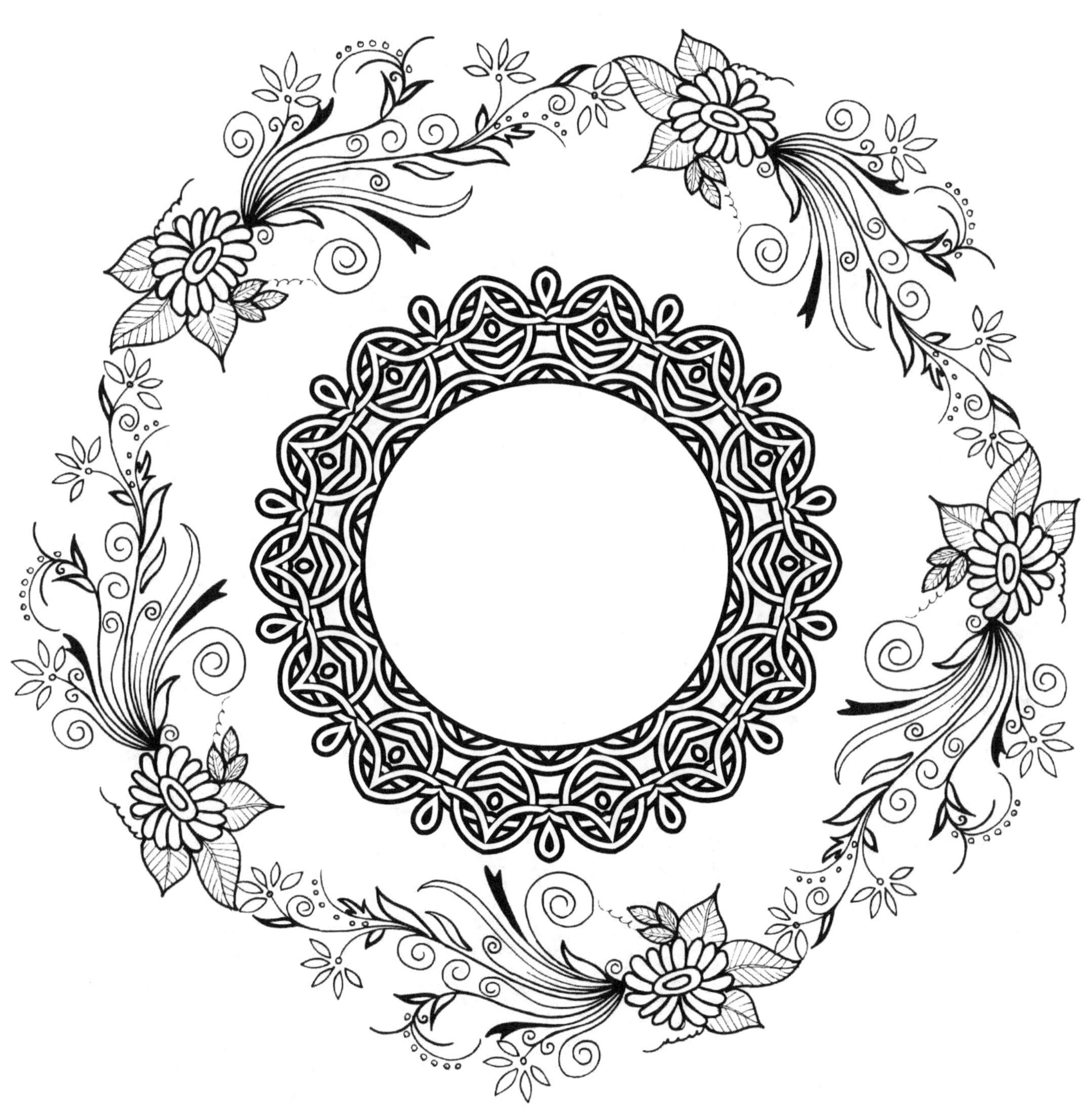

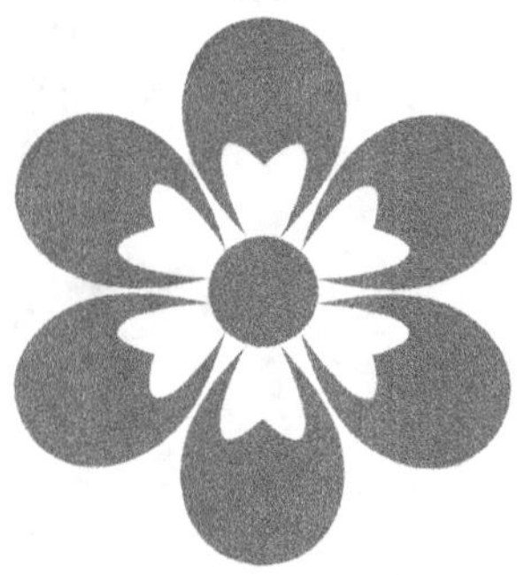

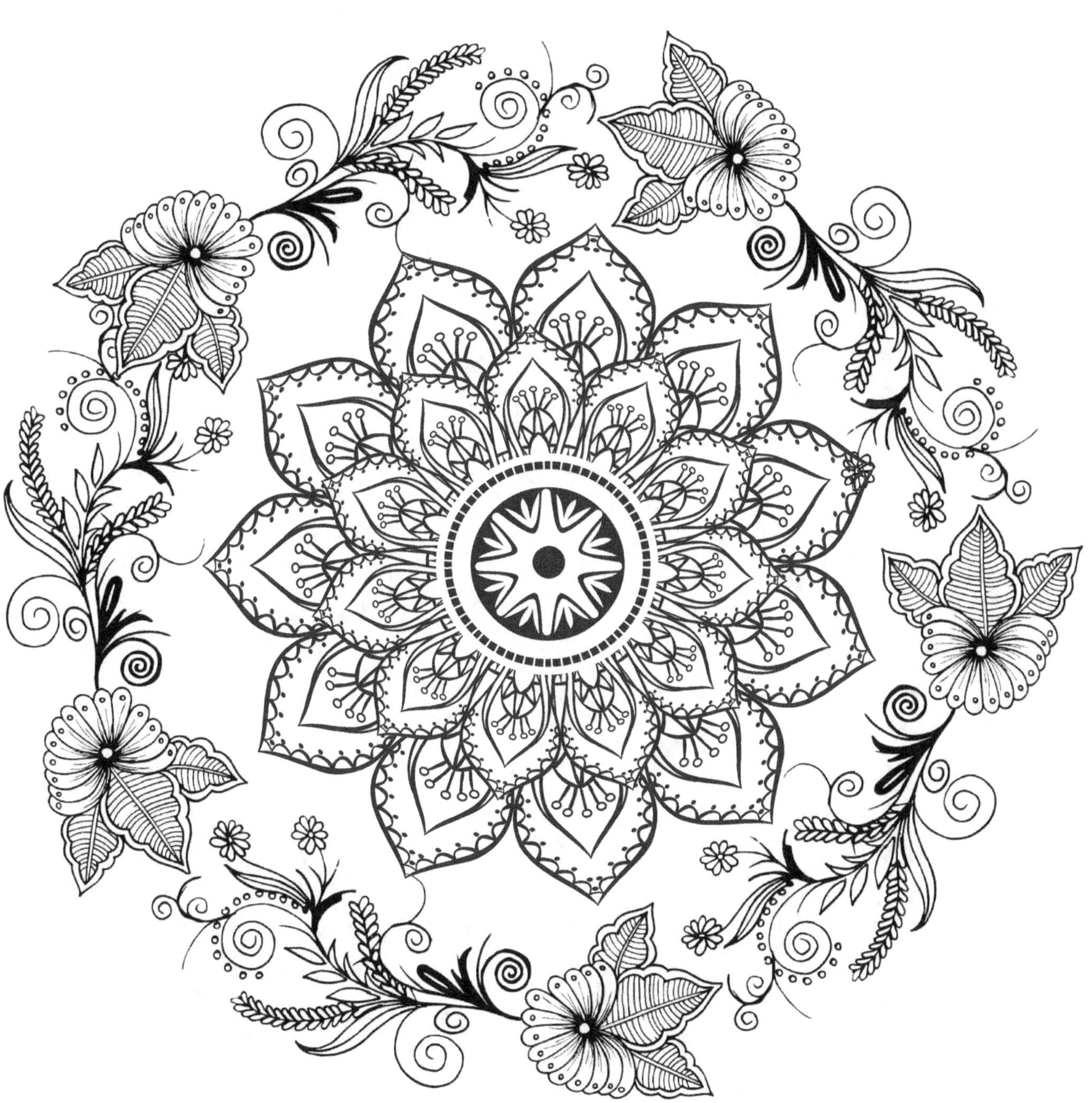

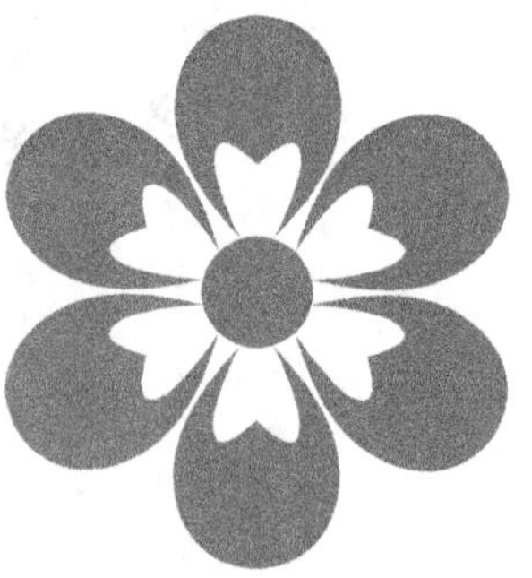

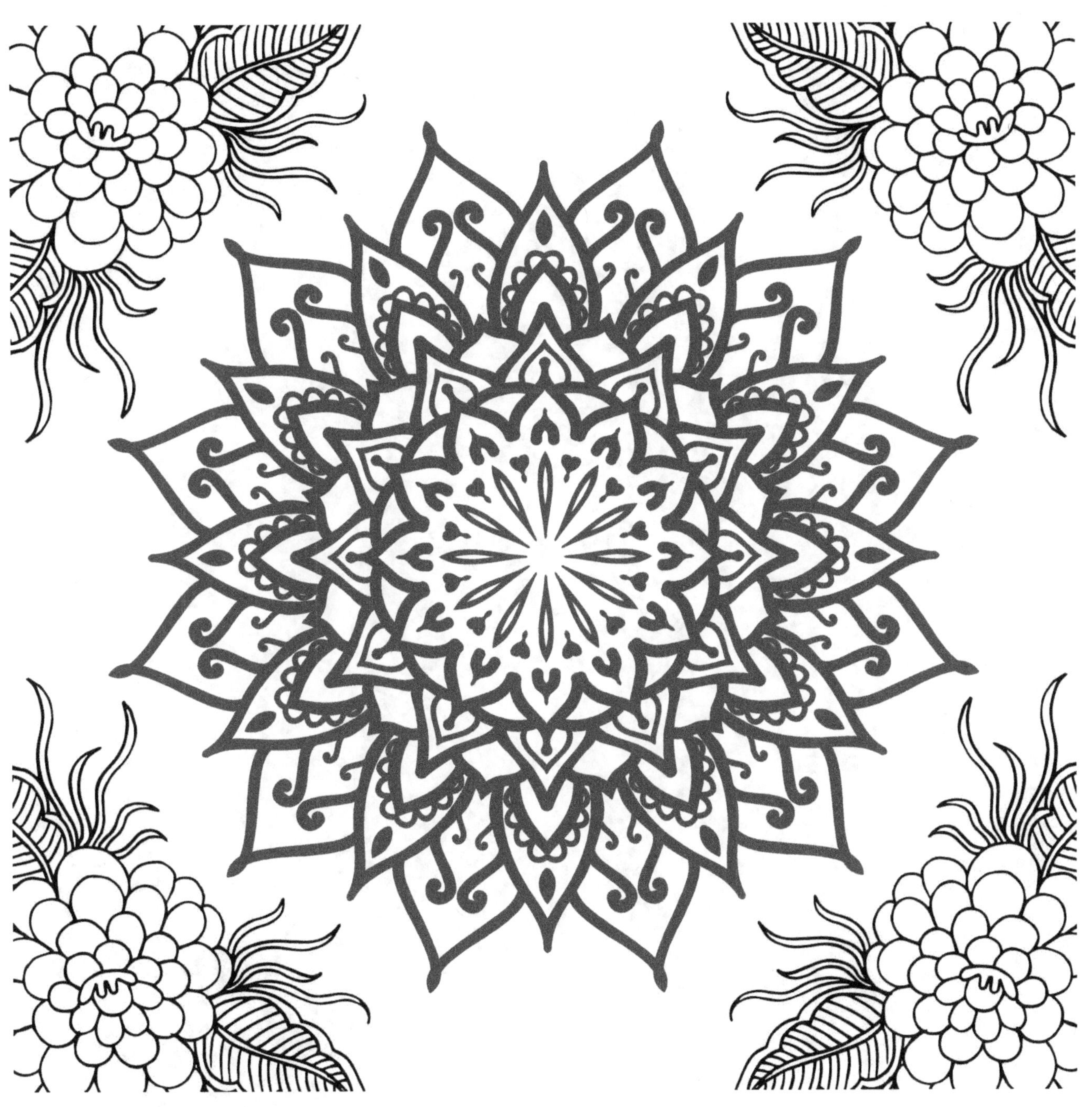

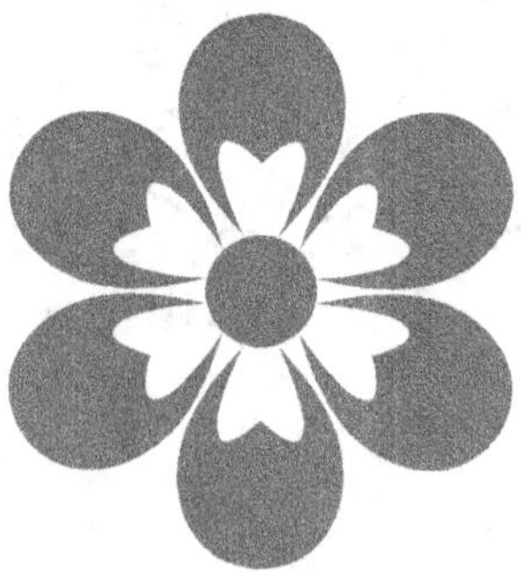

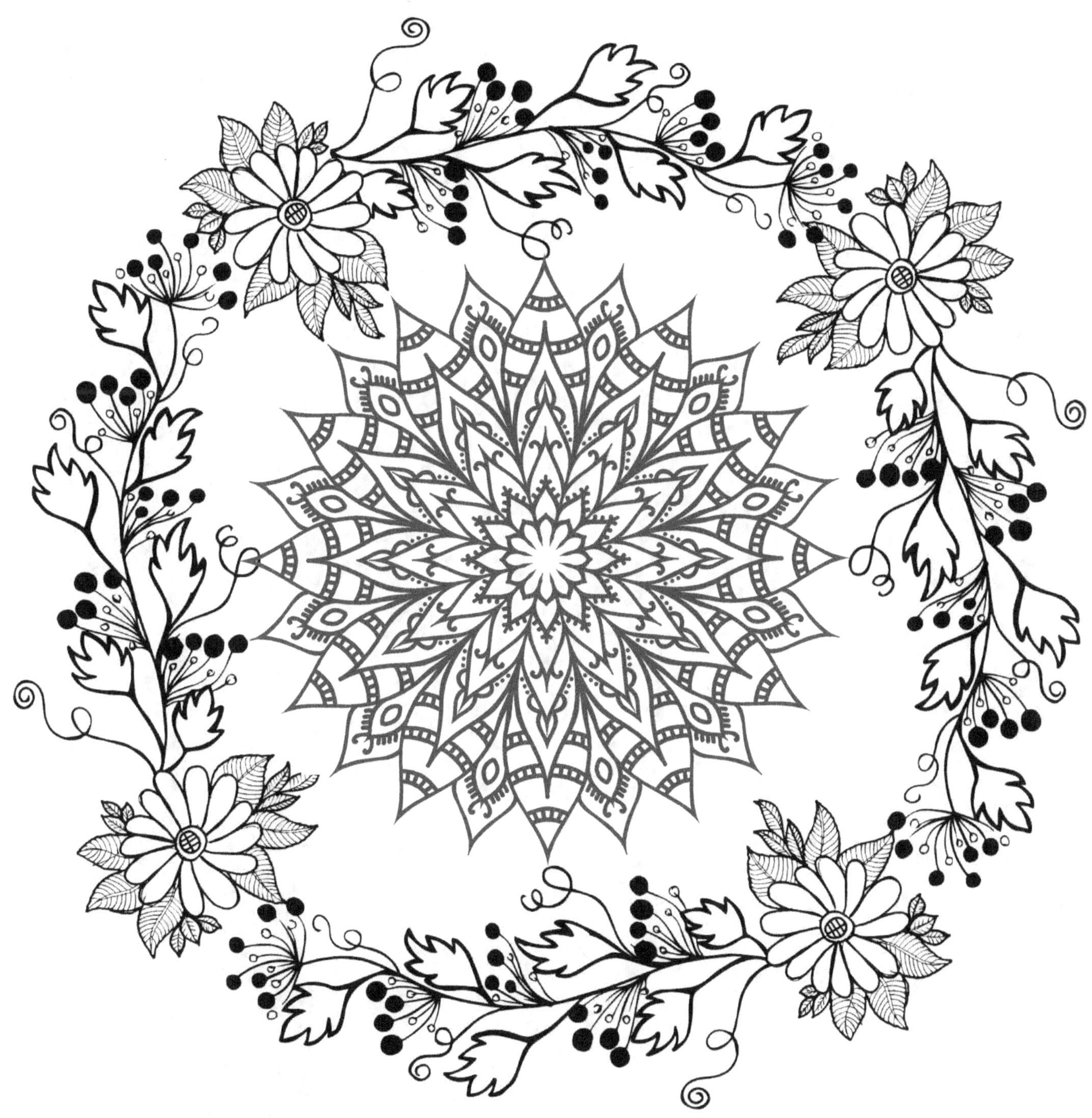

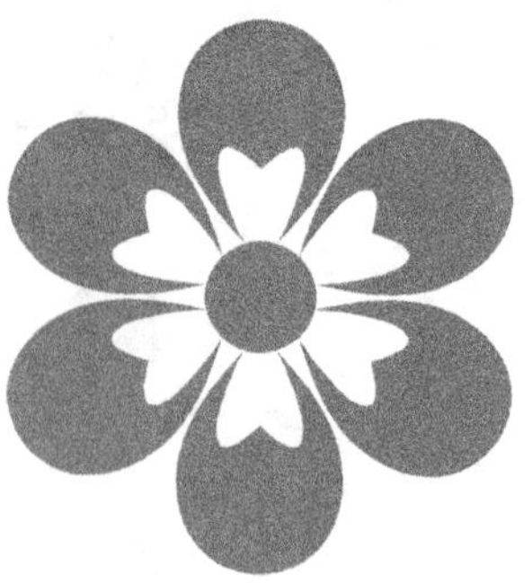

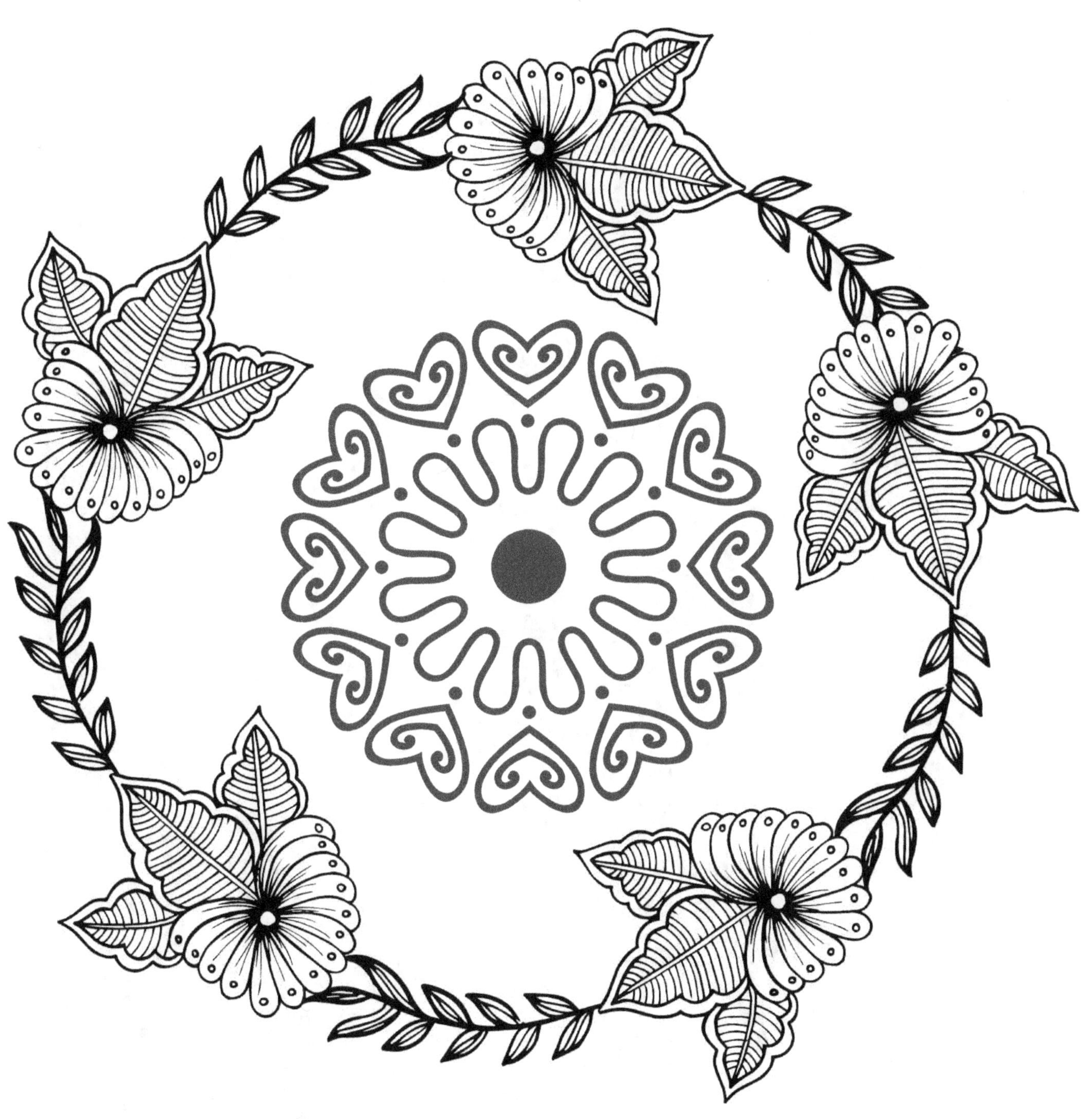

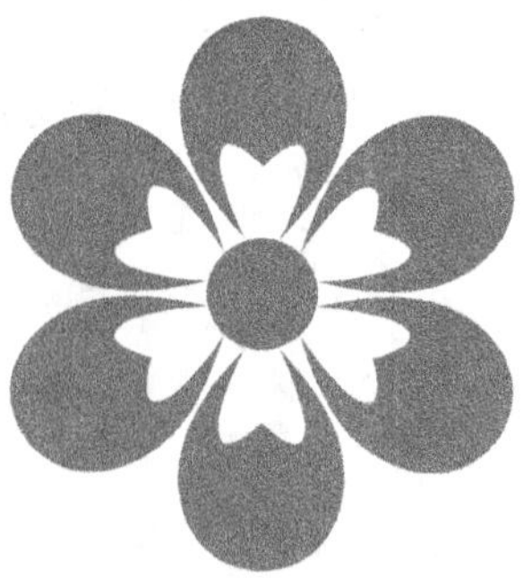

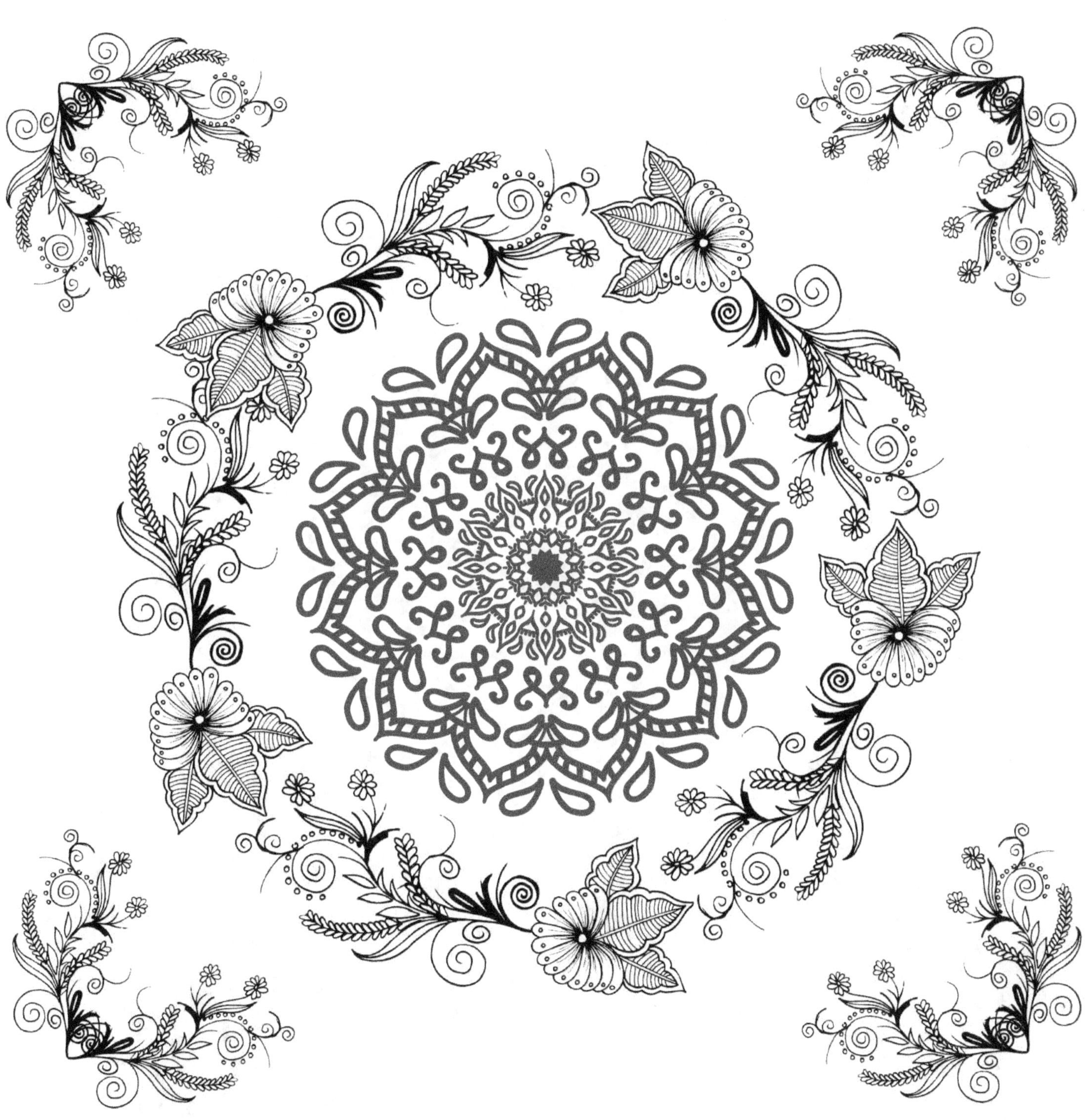

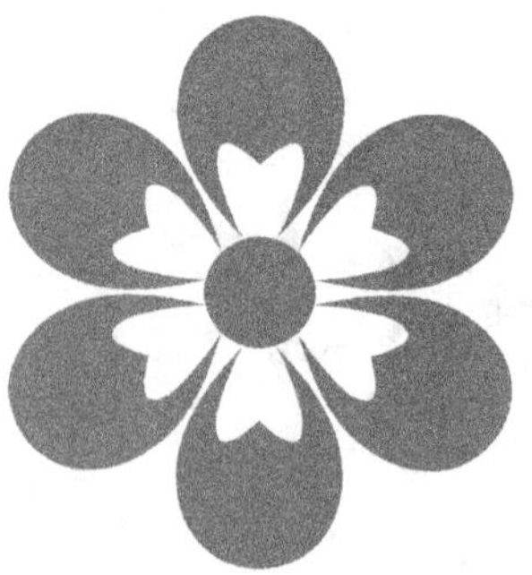

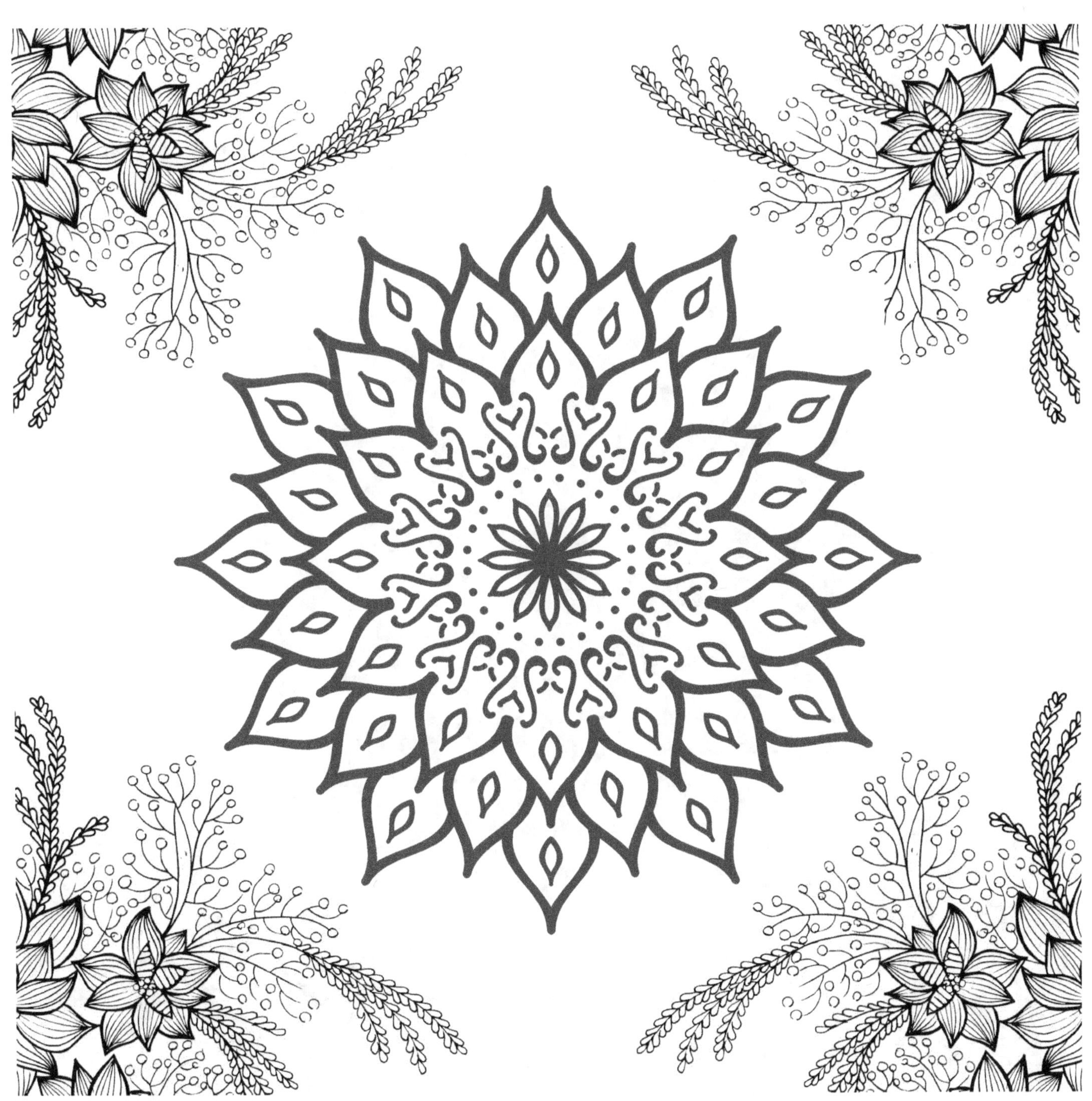

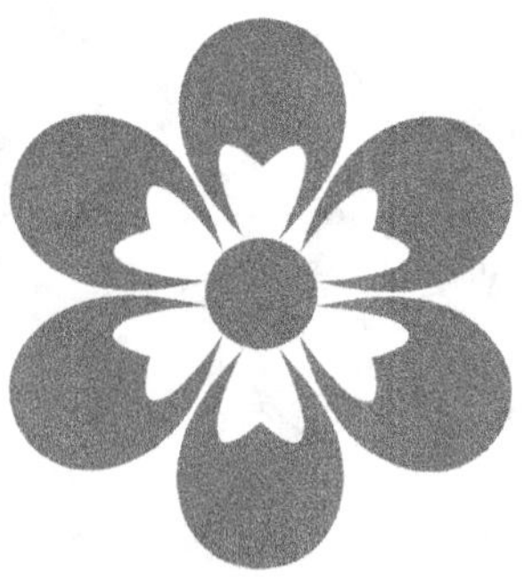

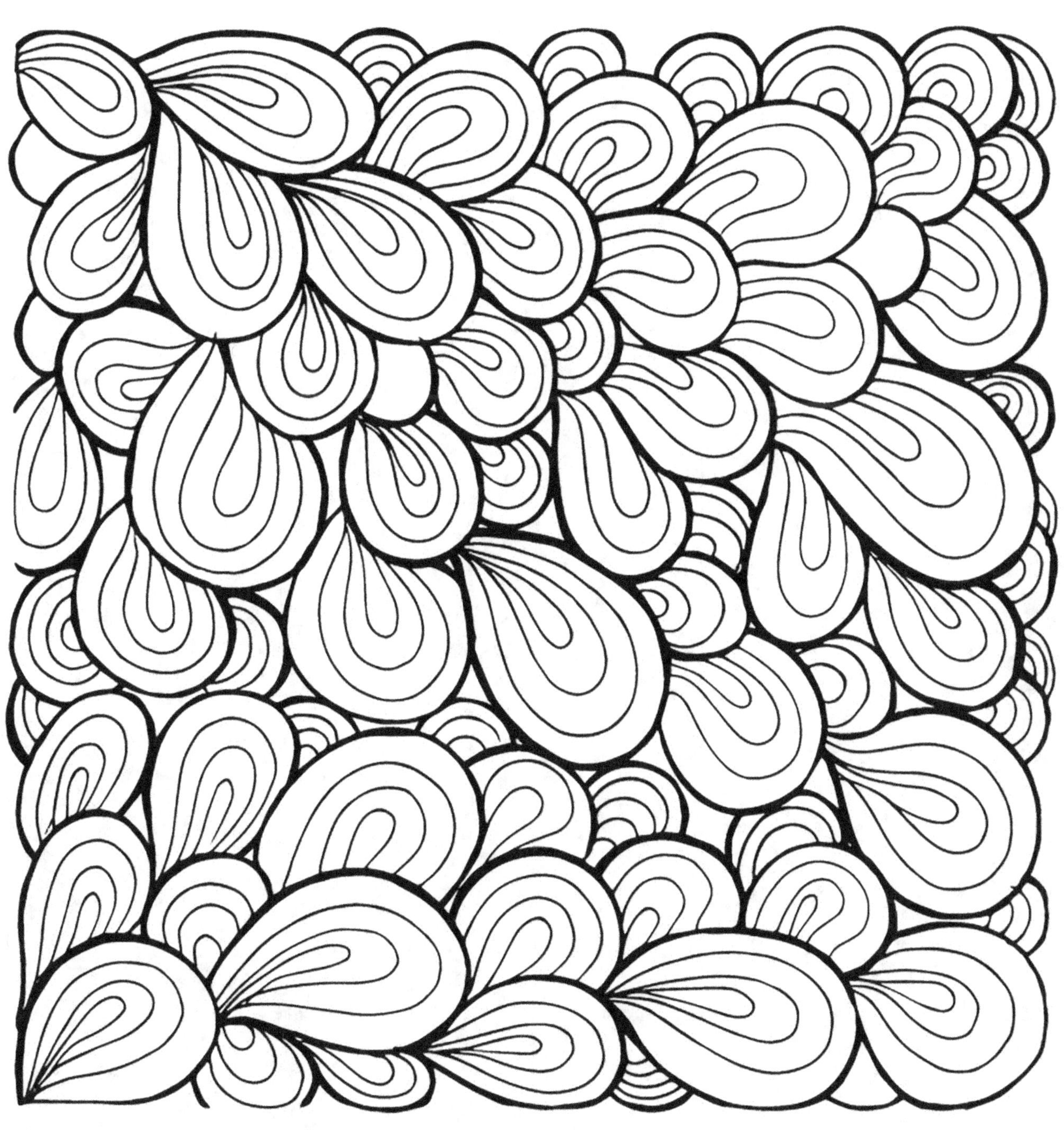

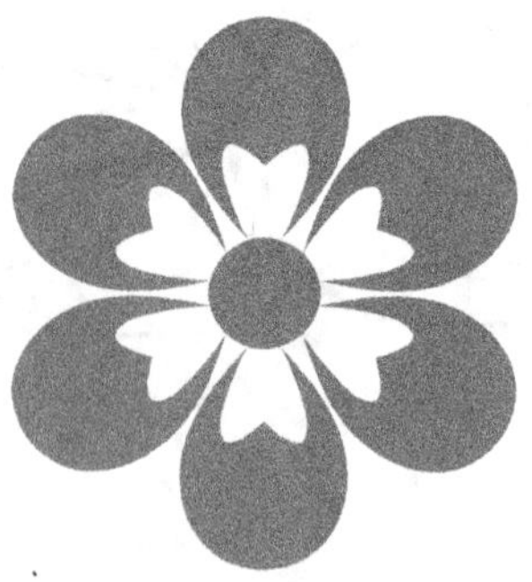

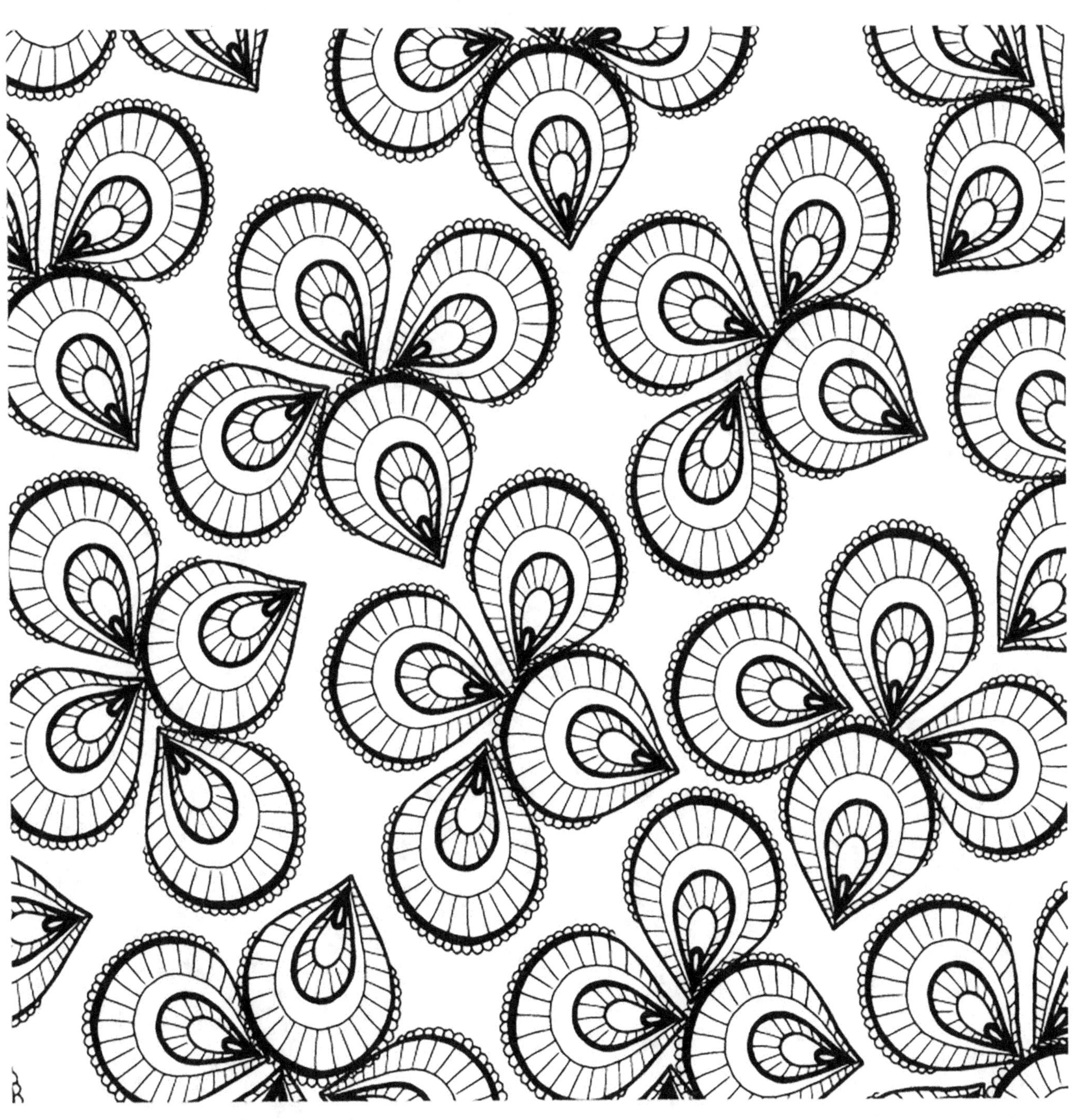

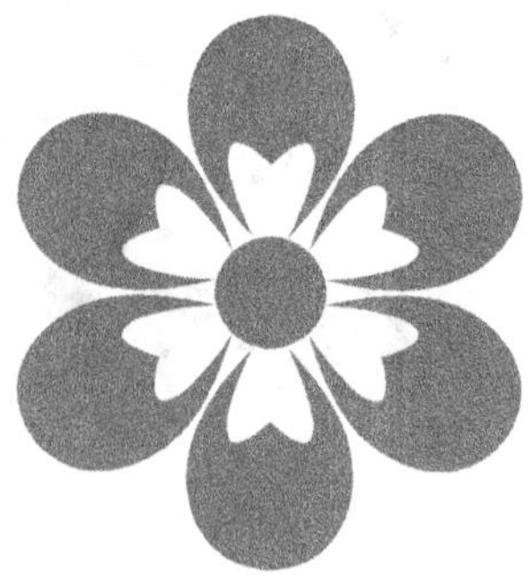

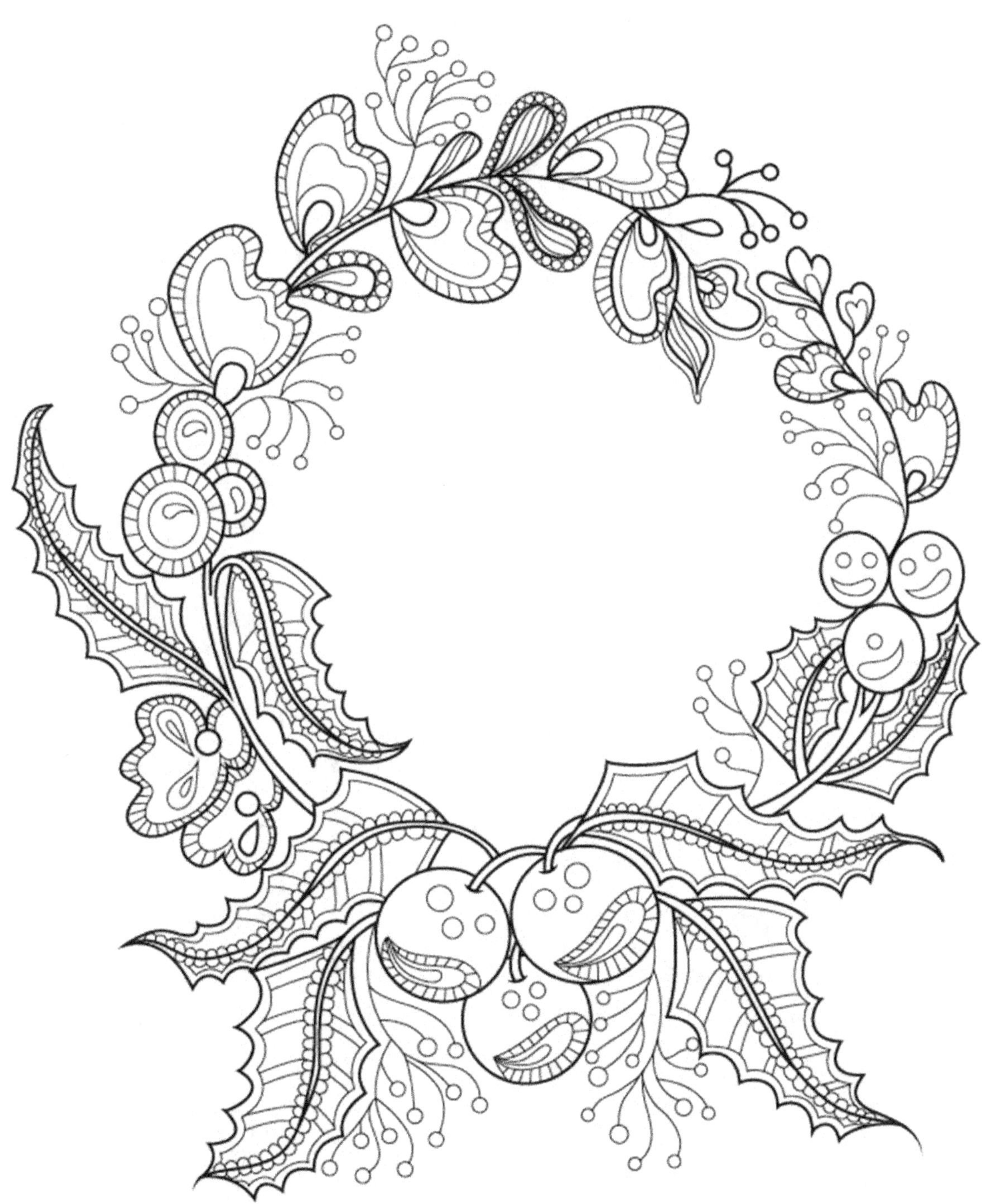

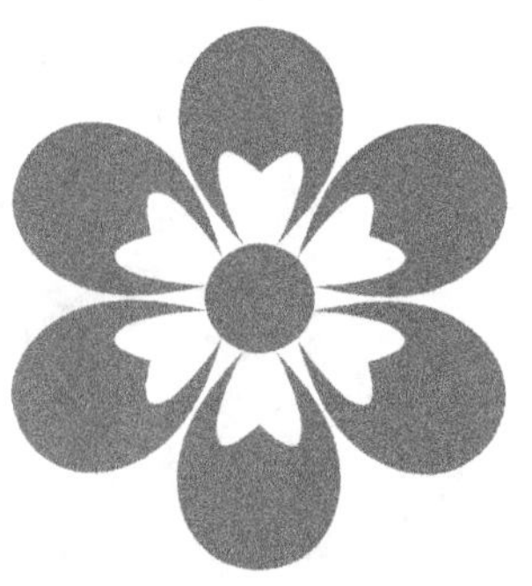

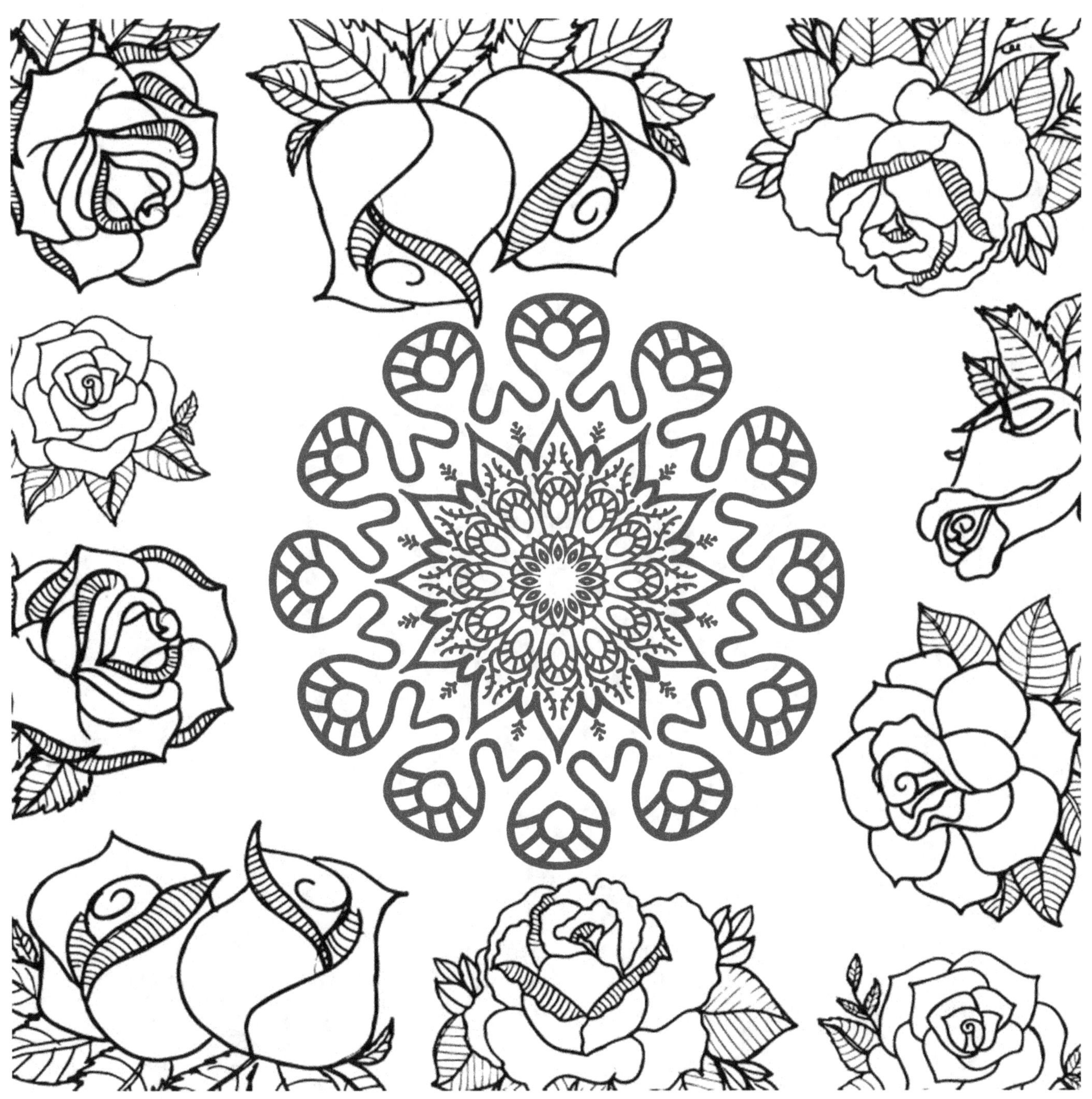

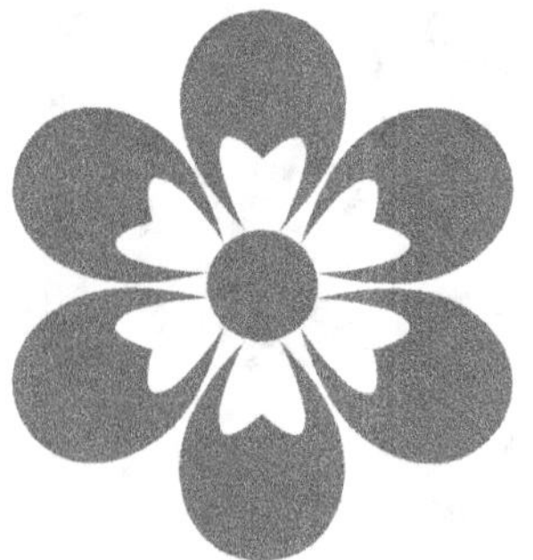

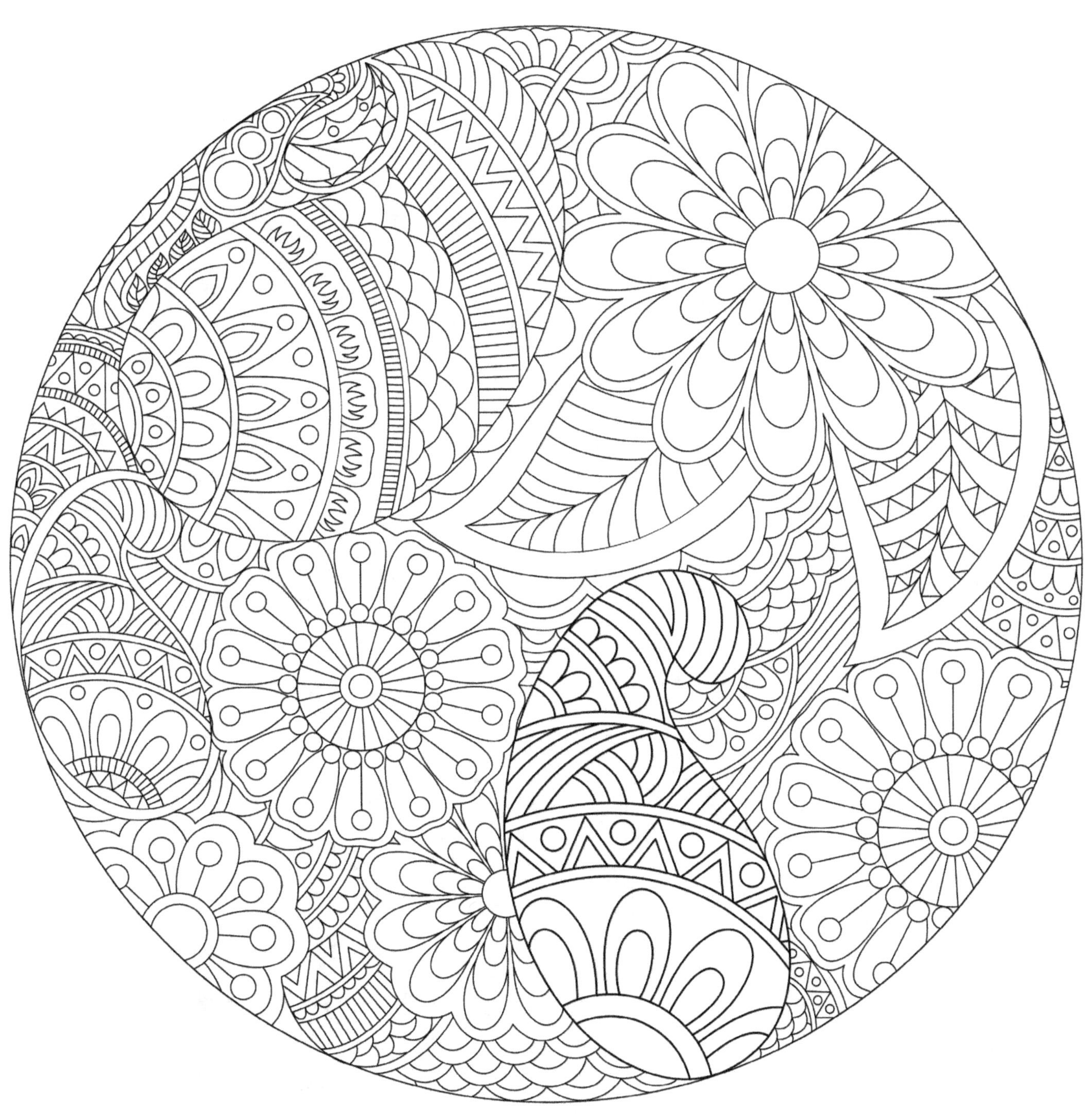

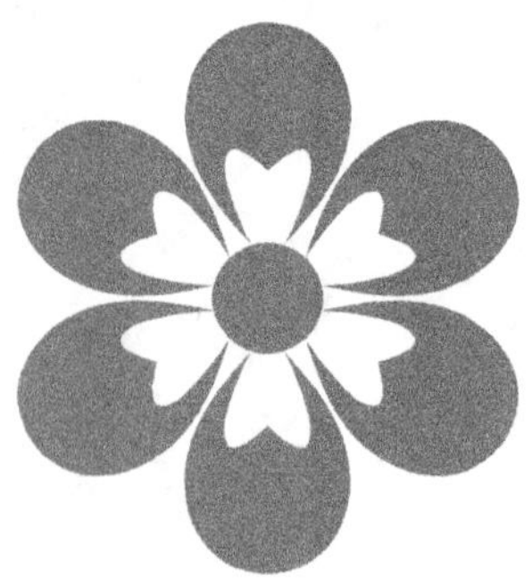

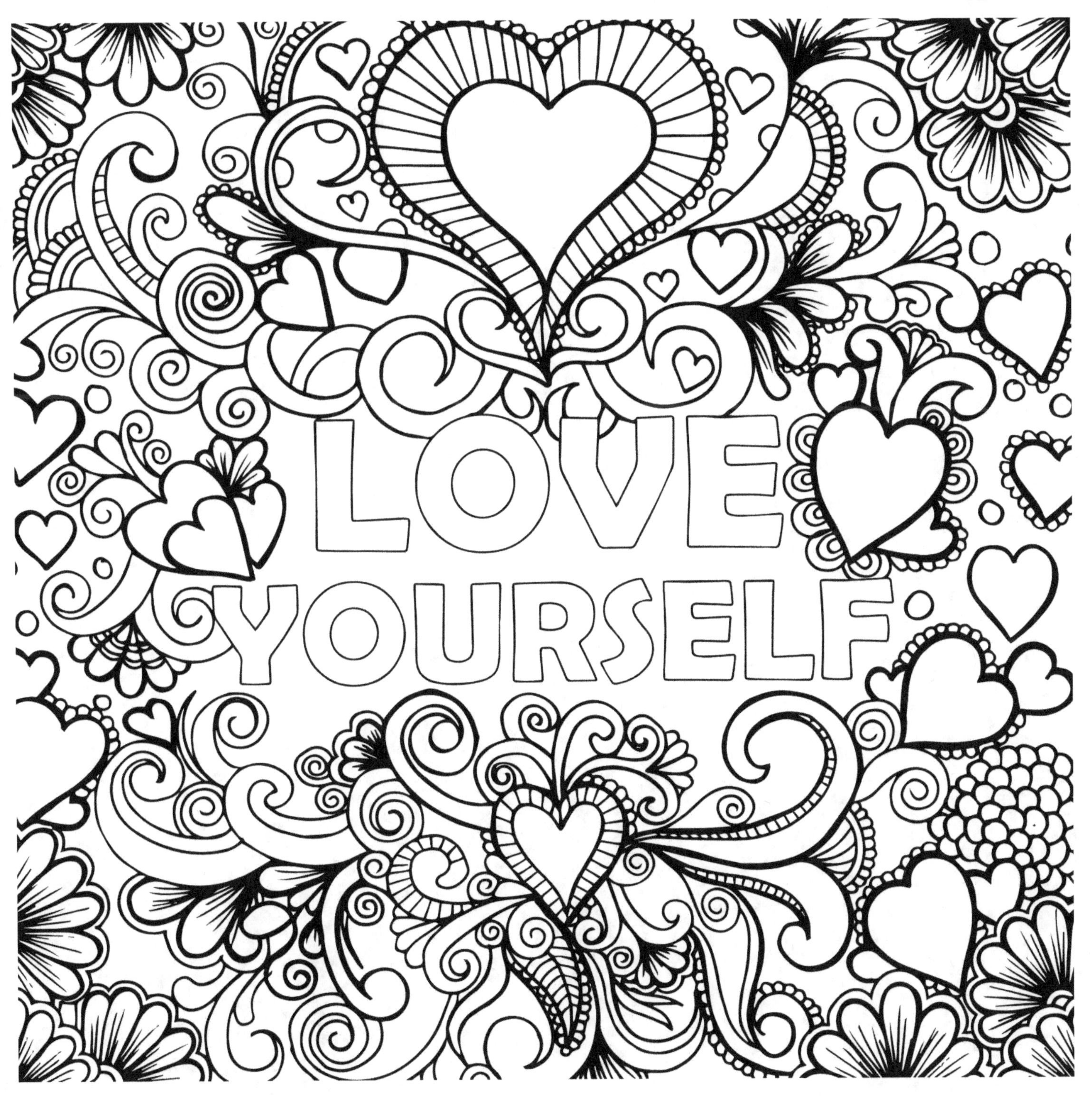

LOVE
YOURSELF

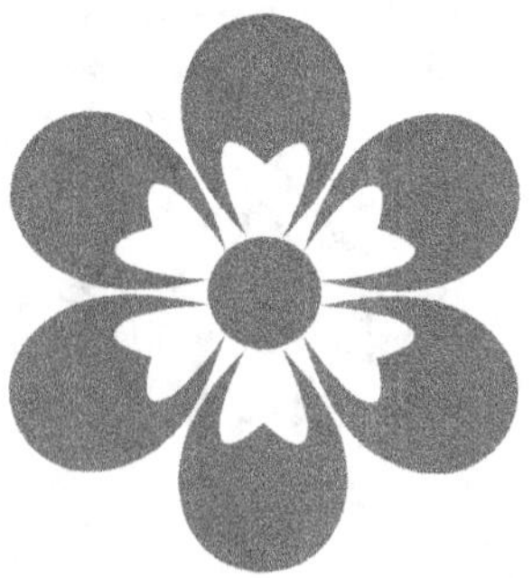

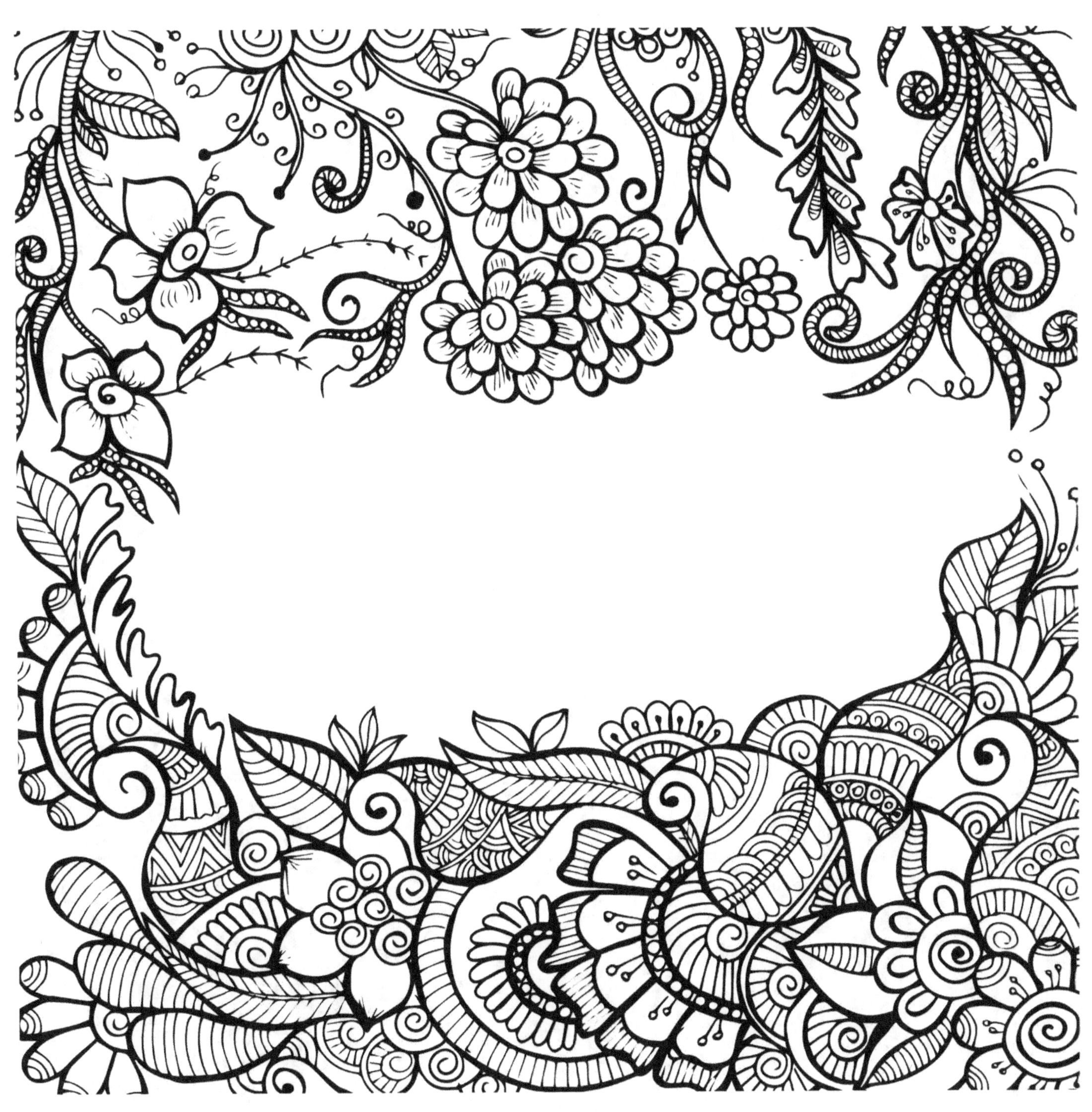

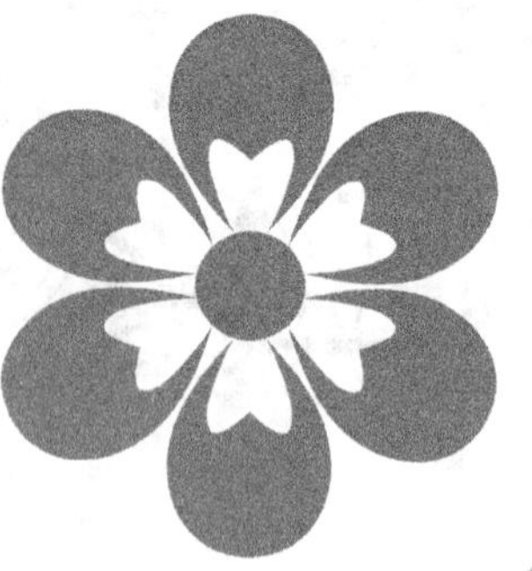

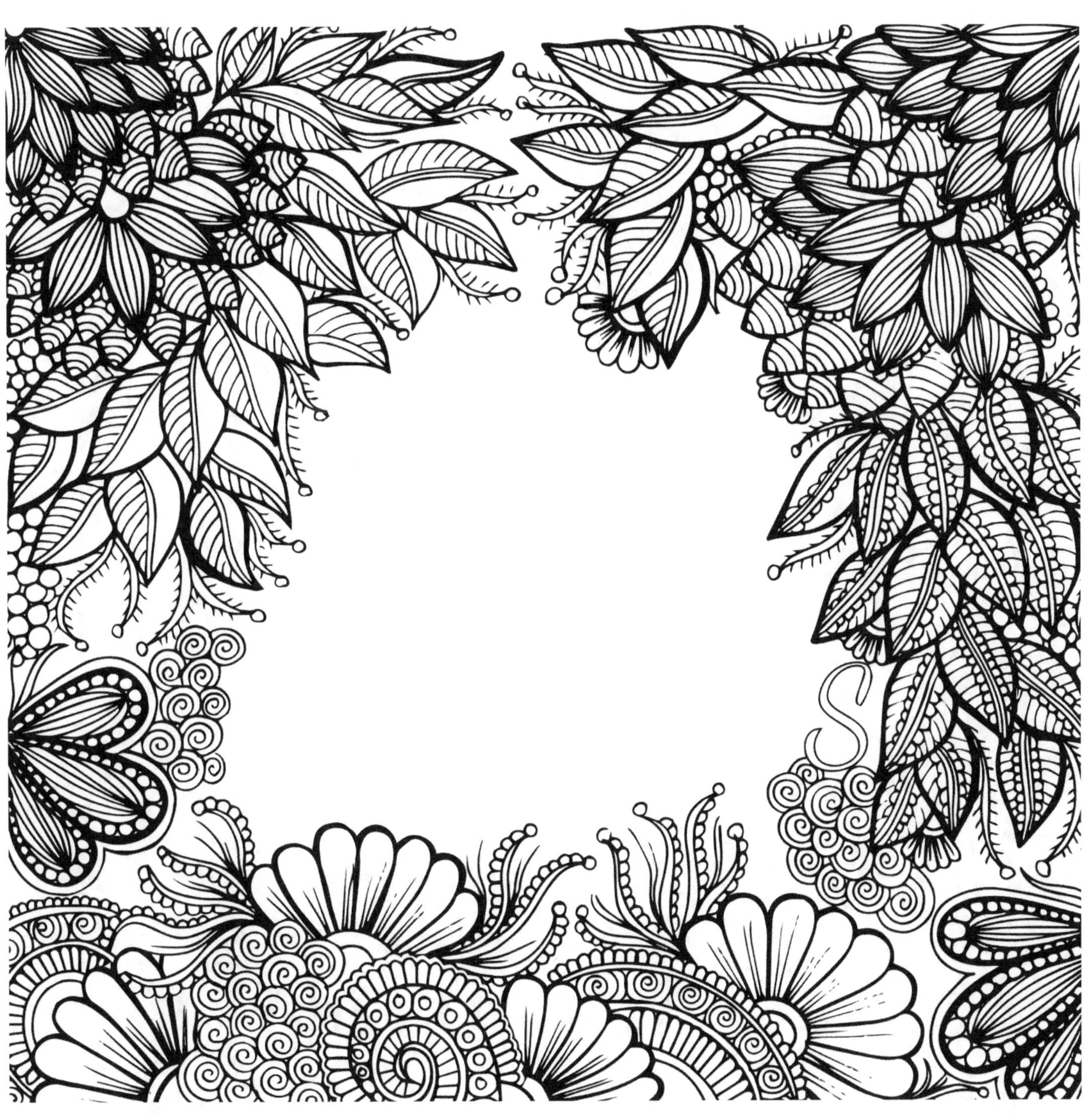

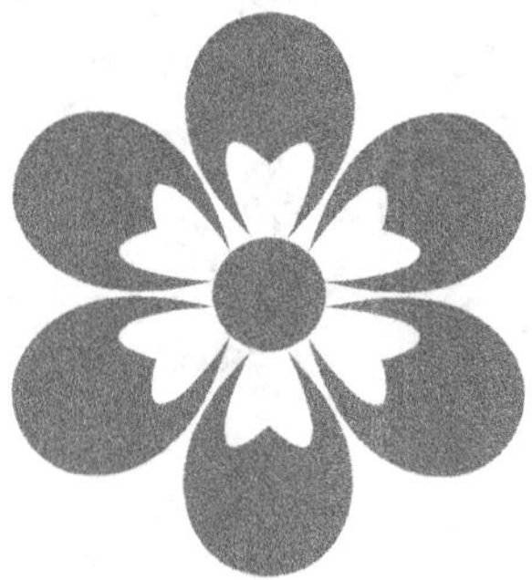

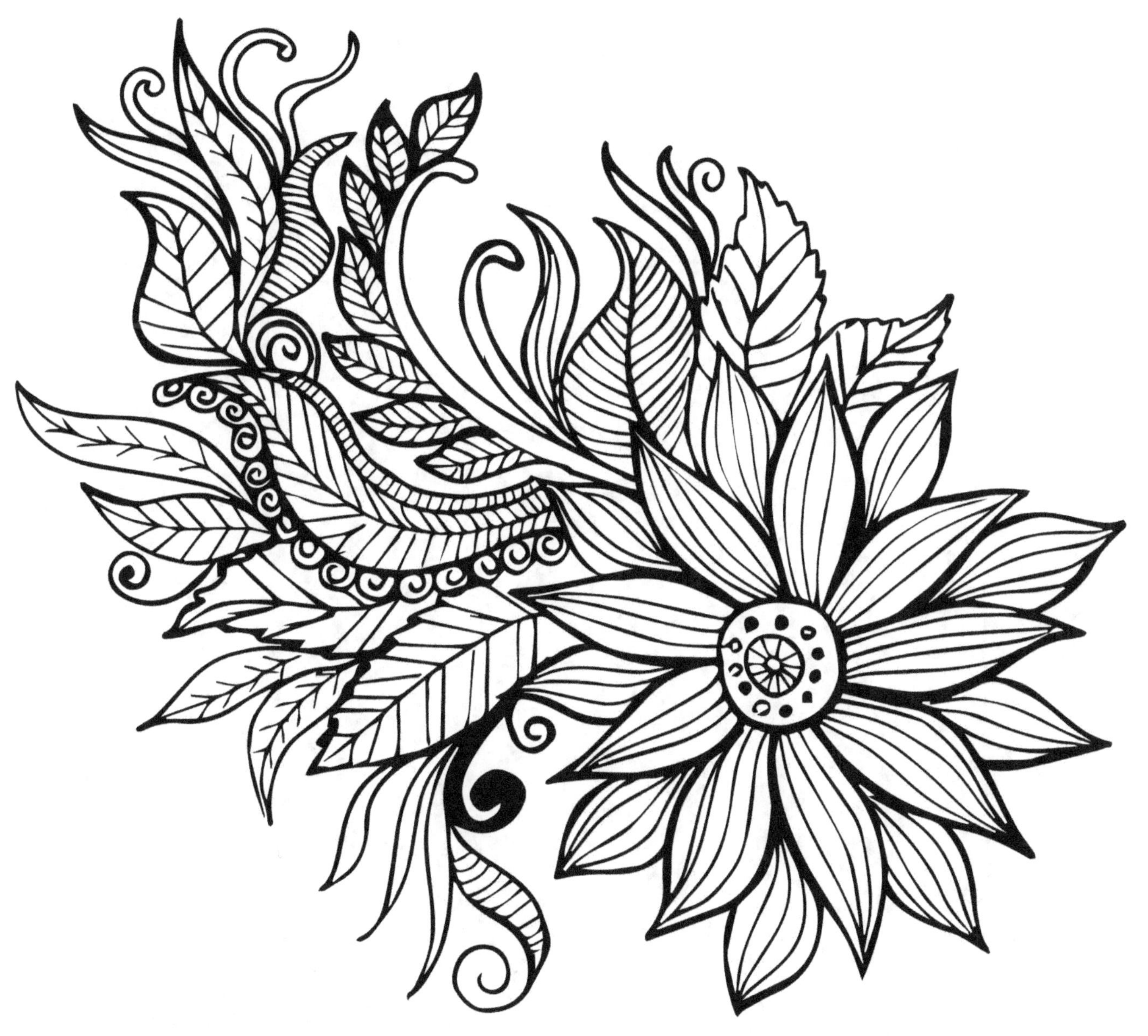

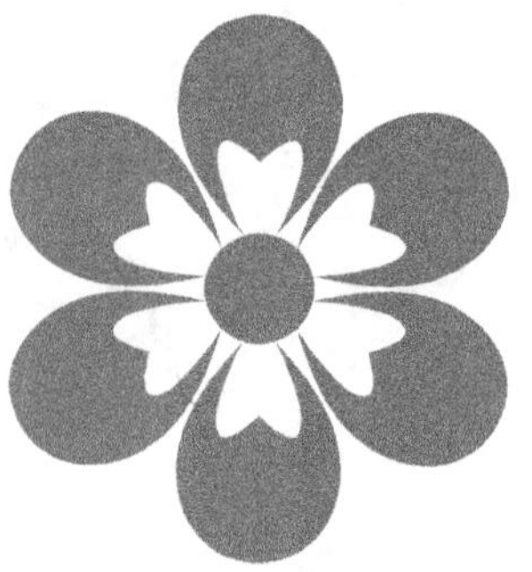

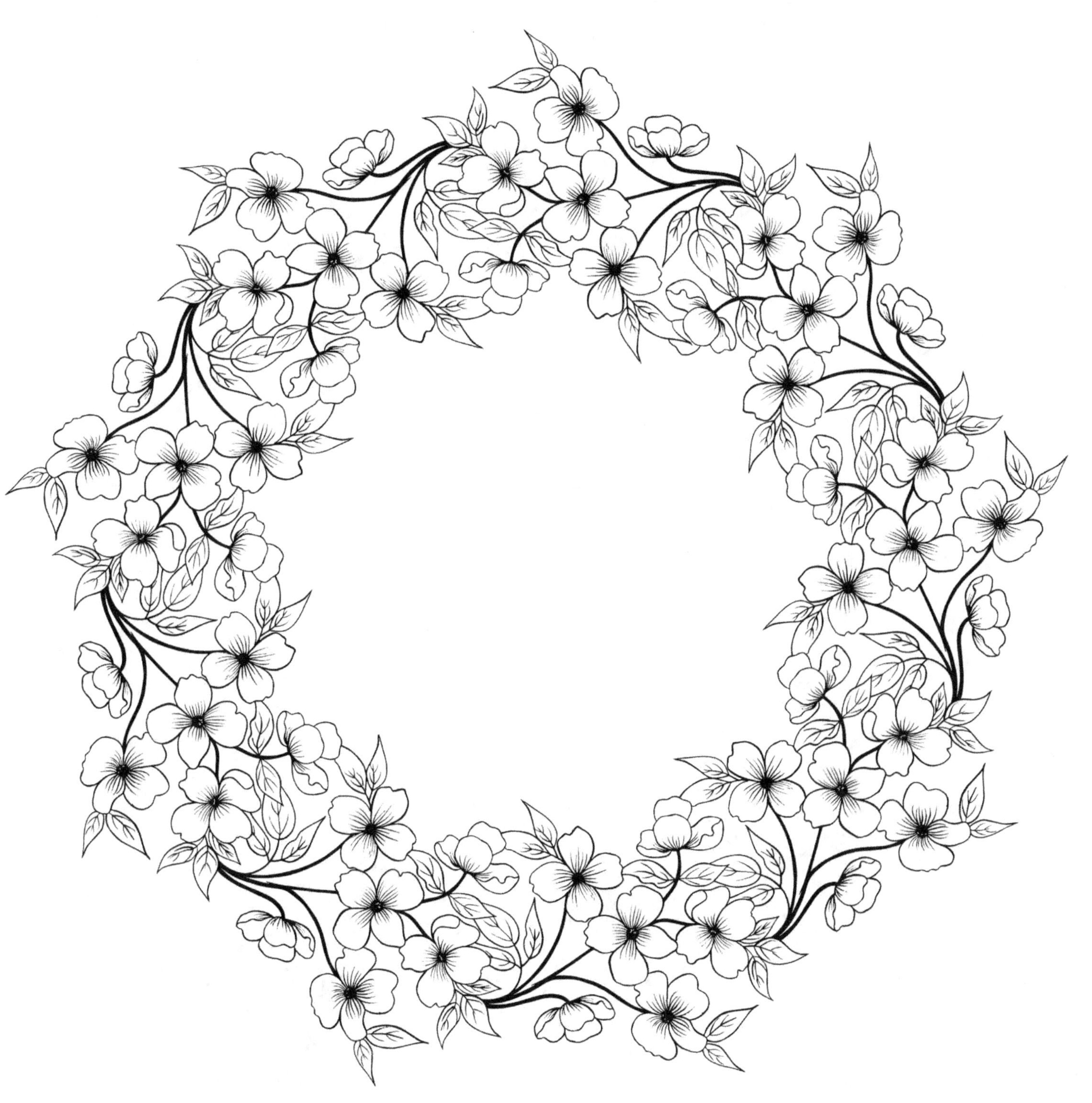

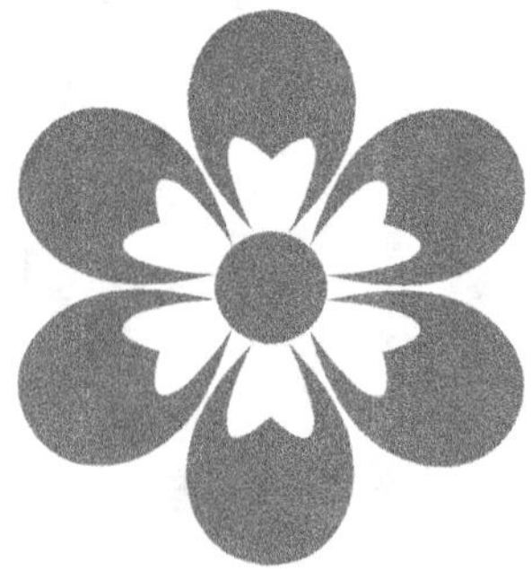

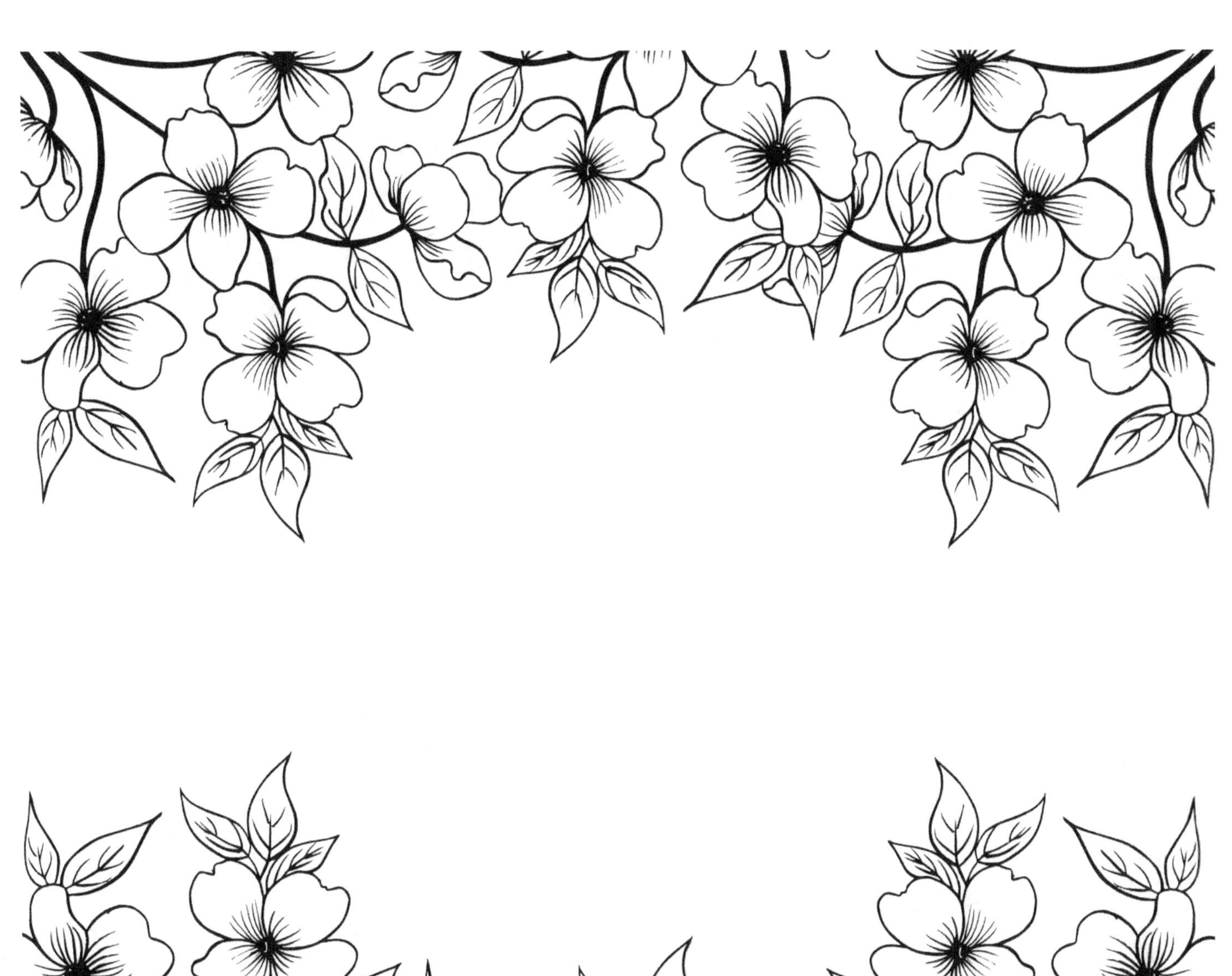

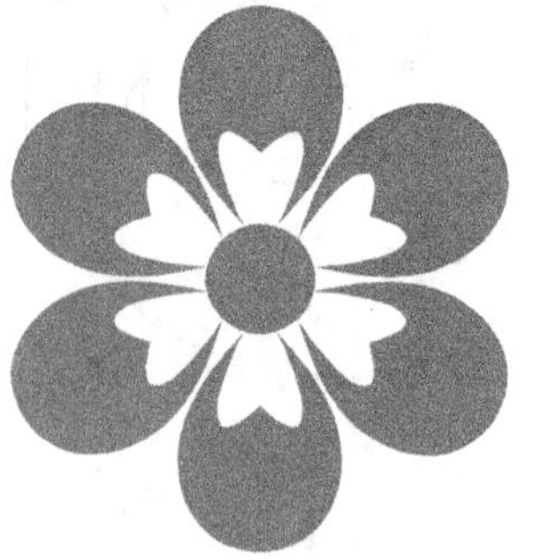

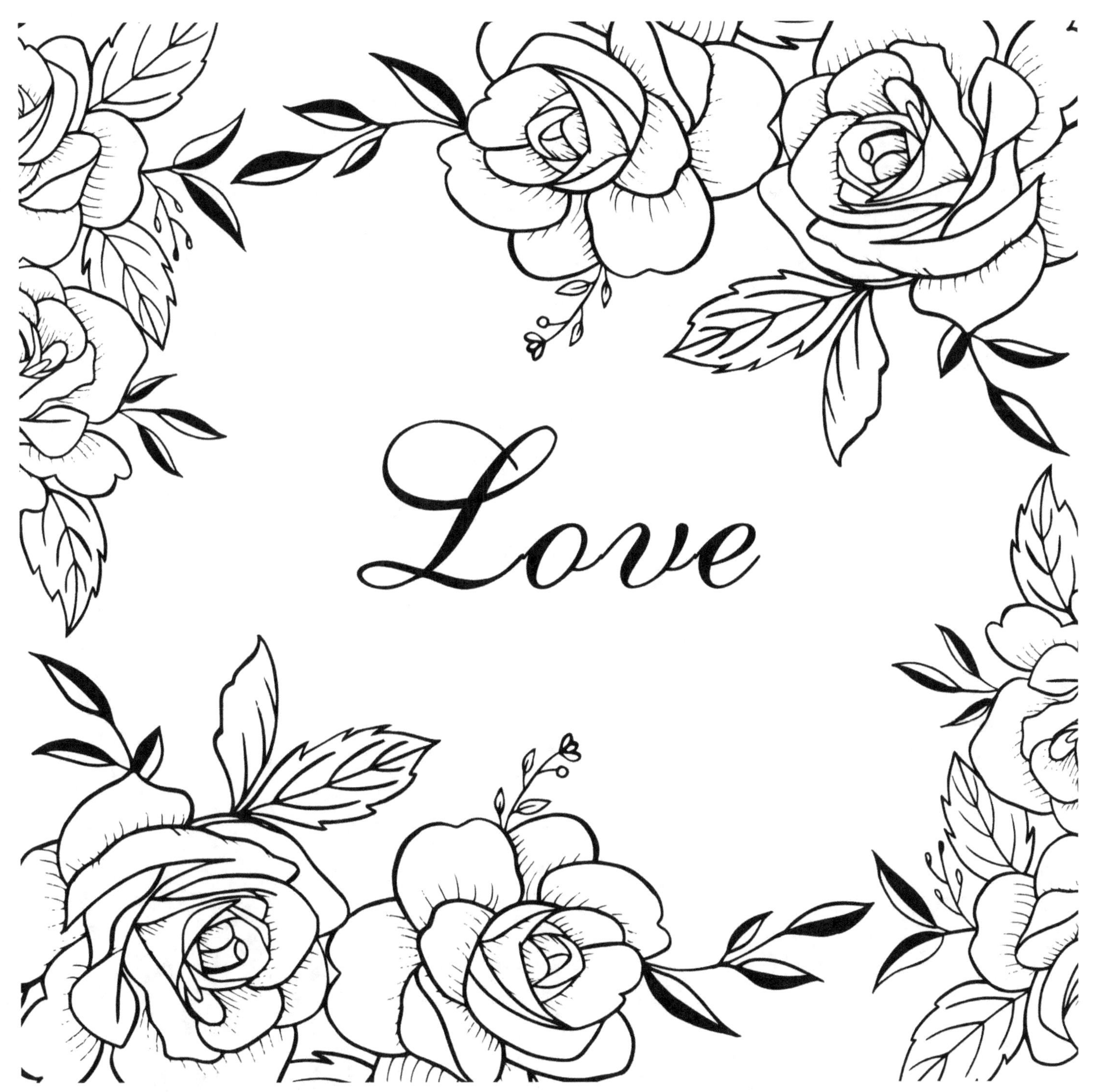
Love

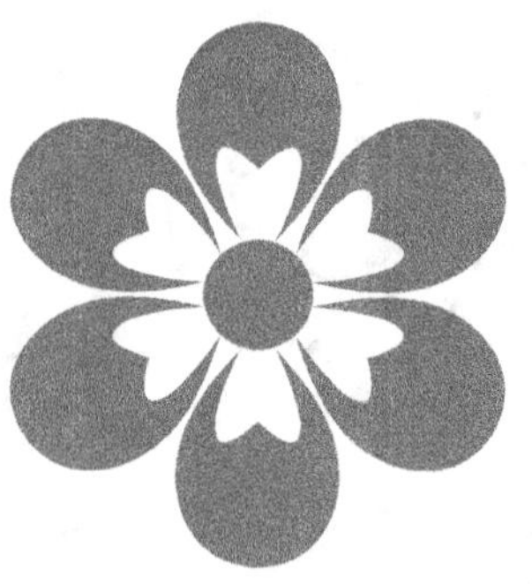

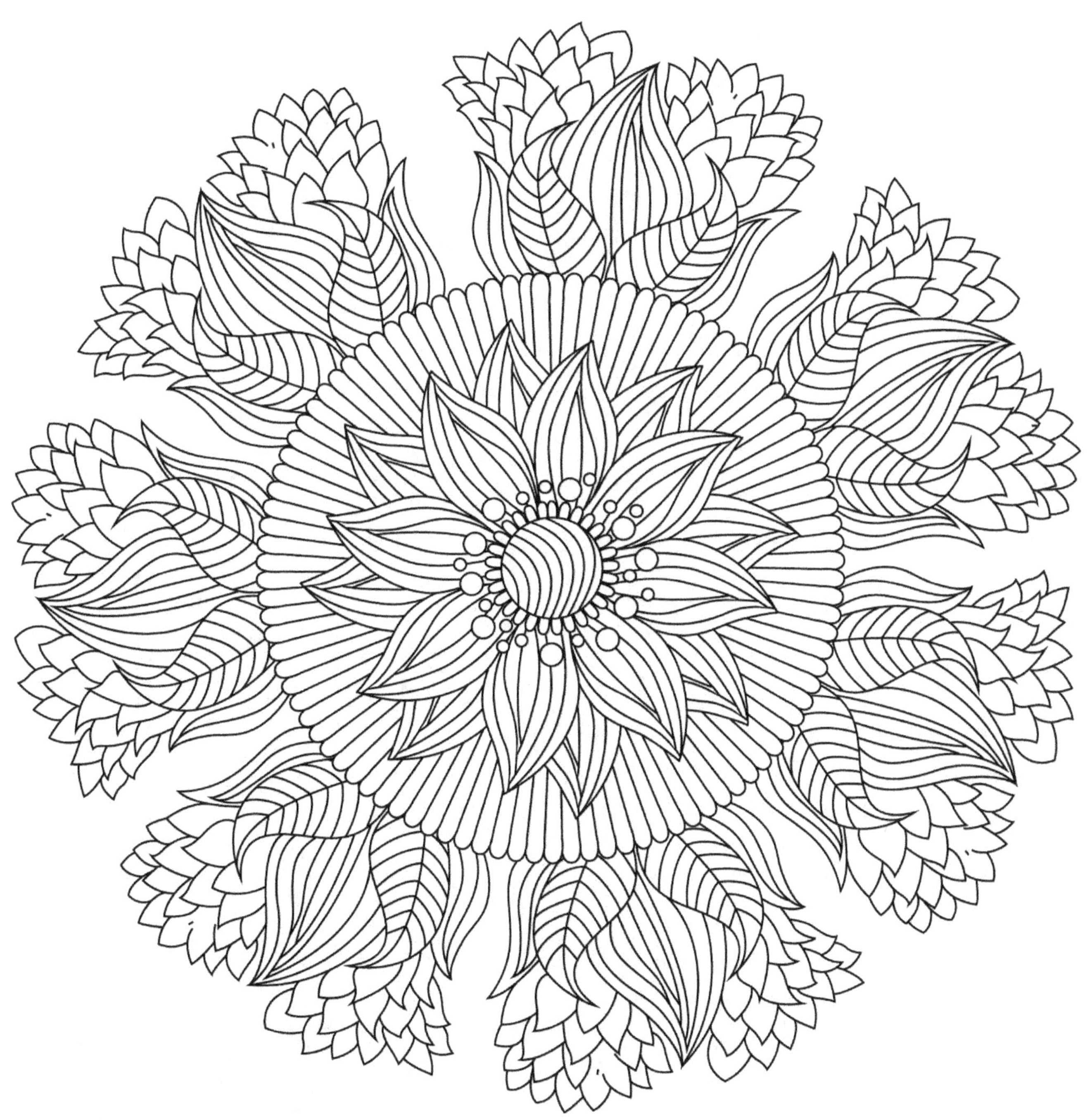

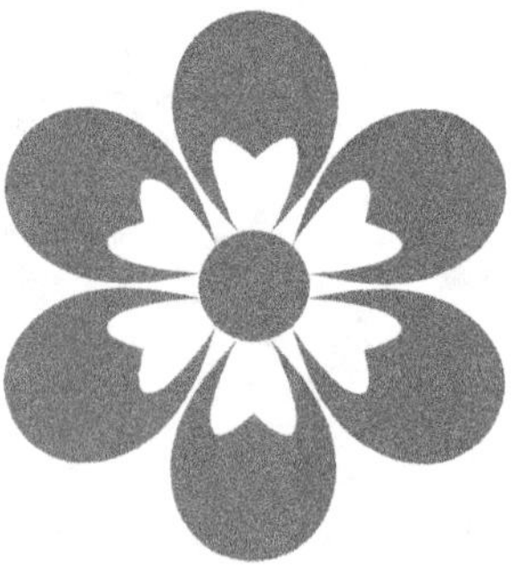

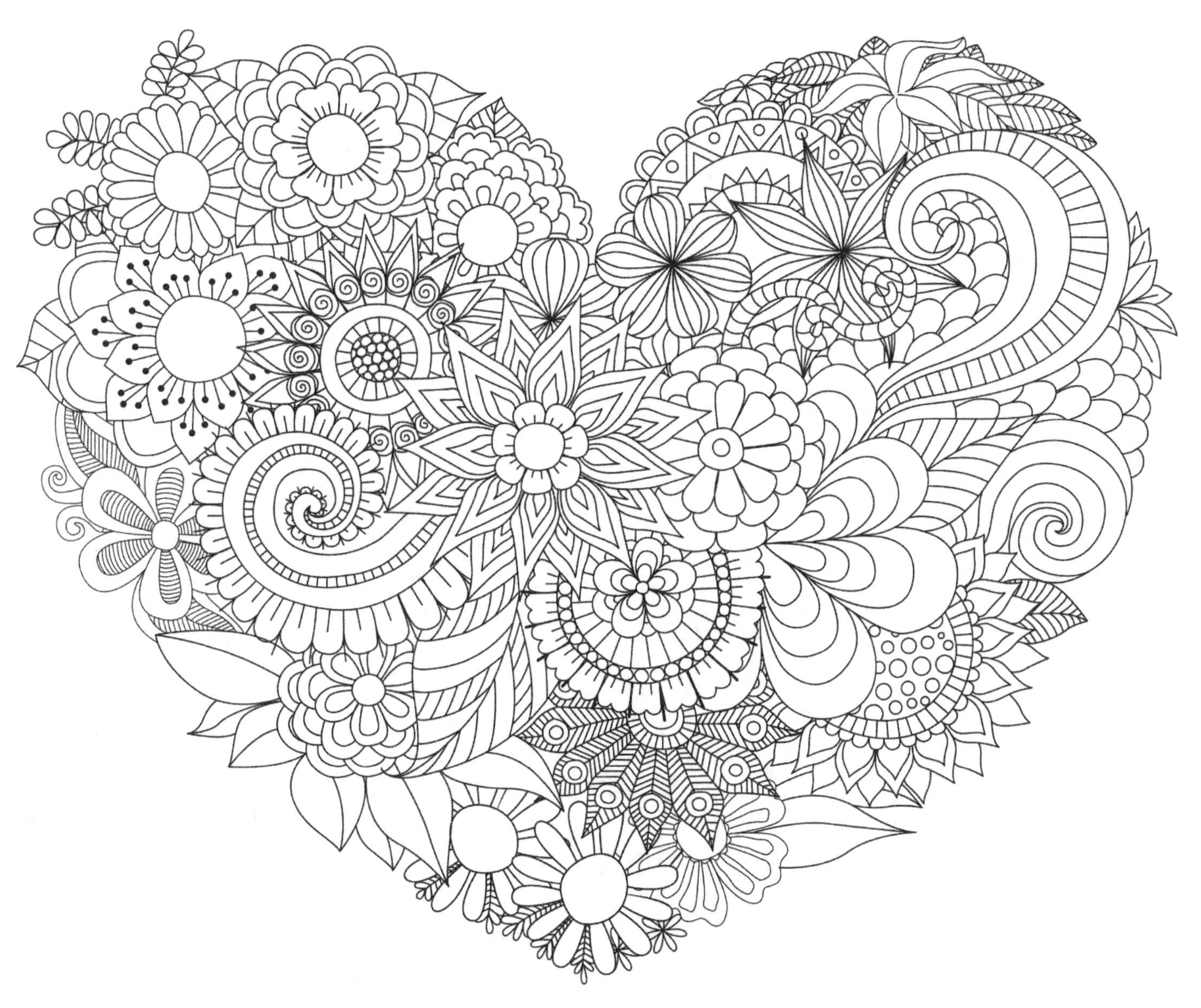

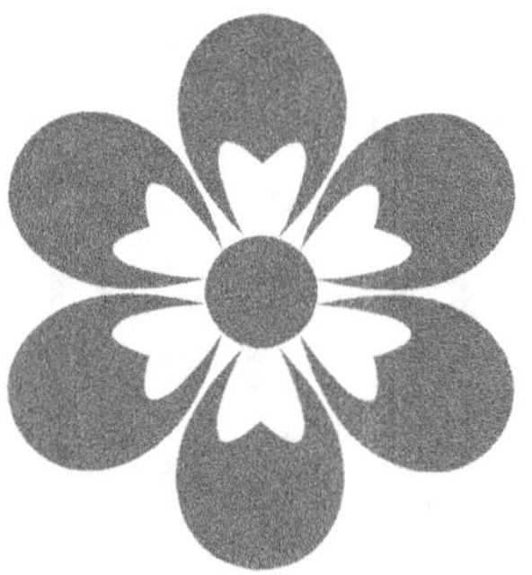

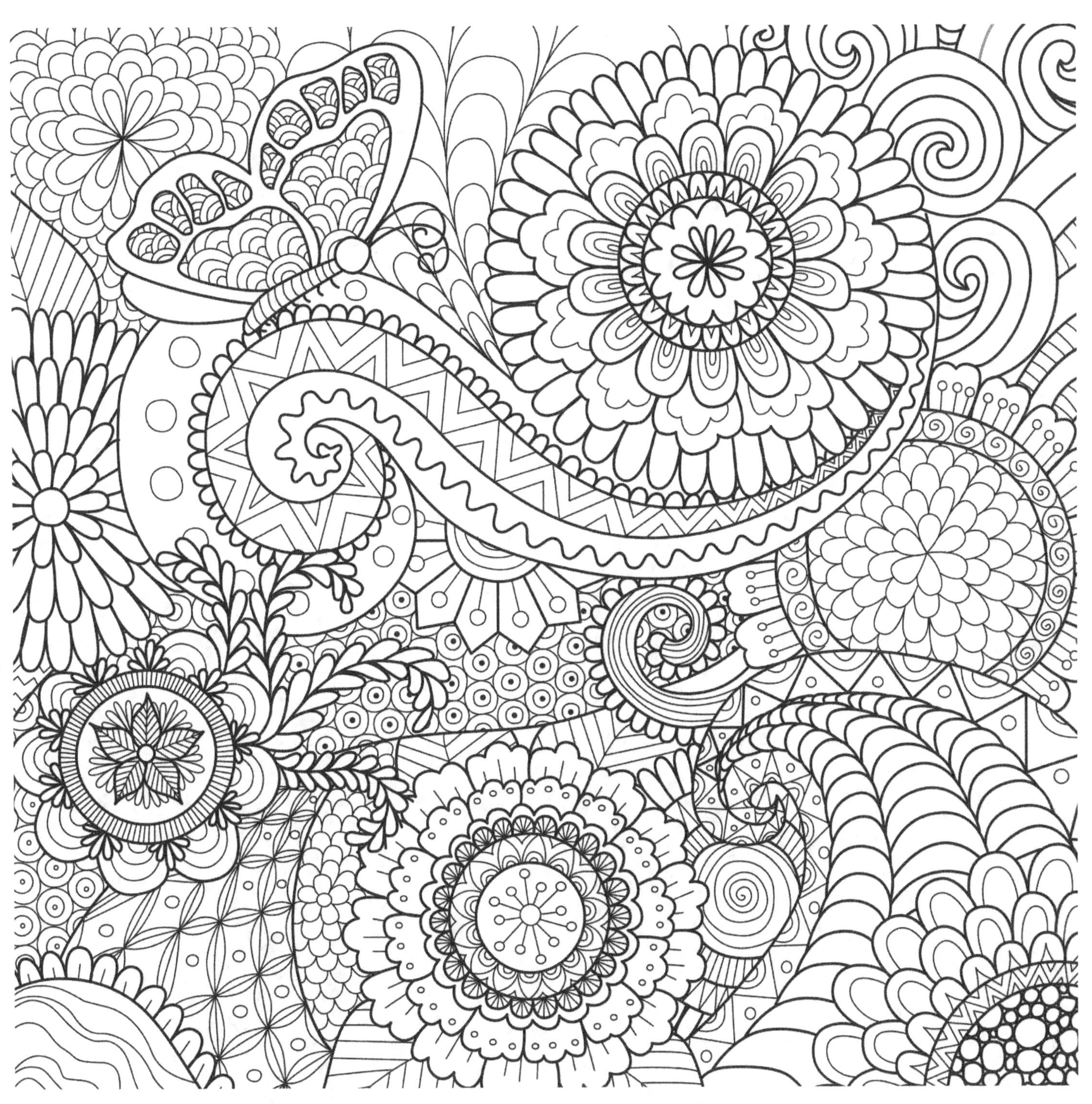

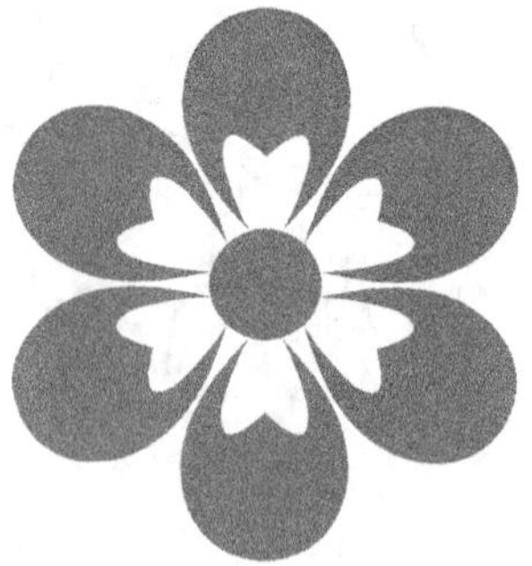

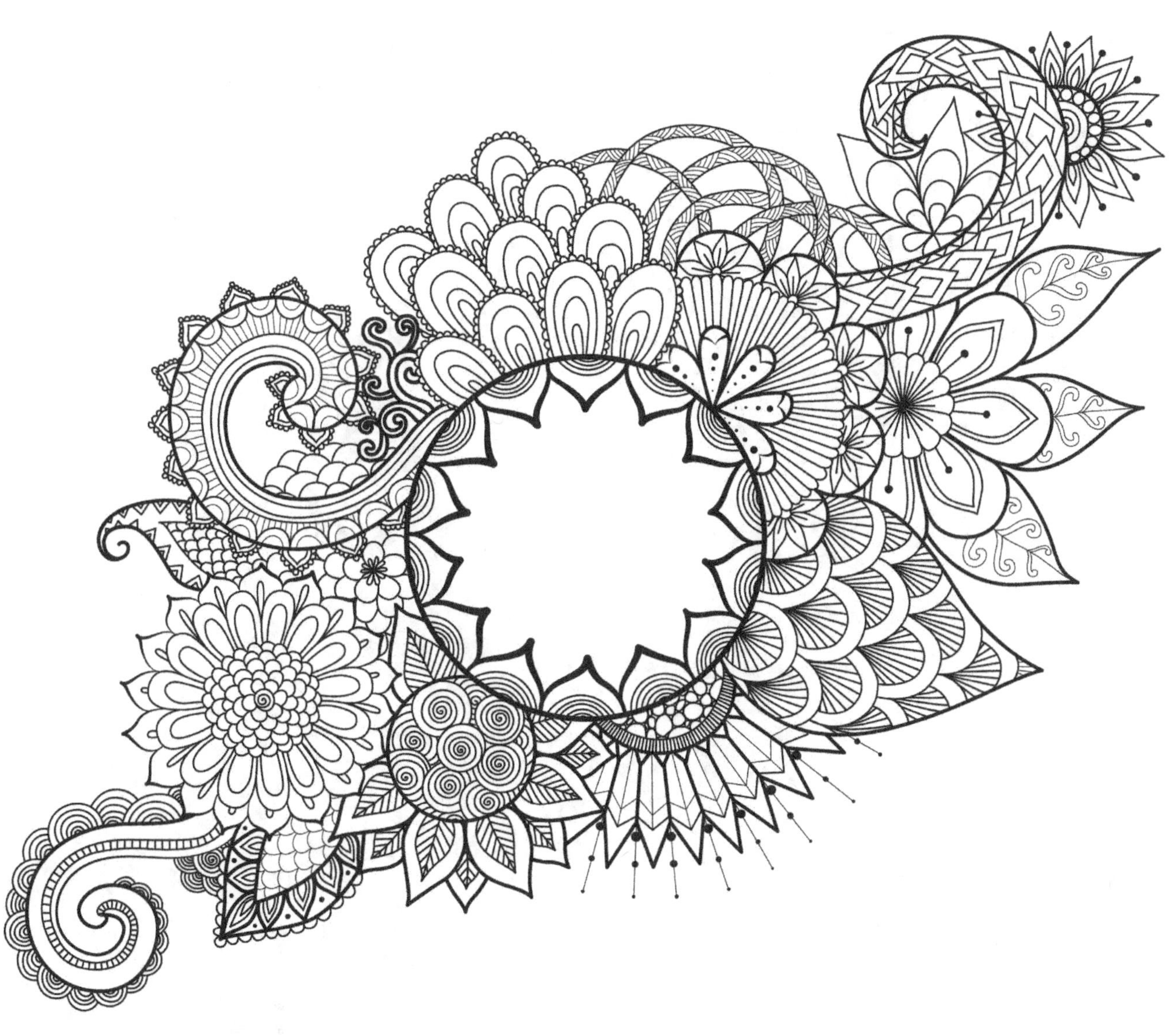

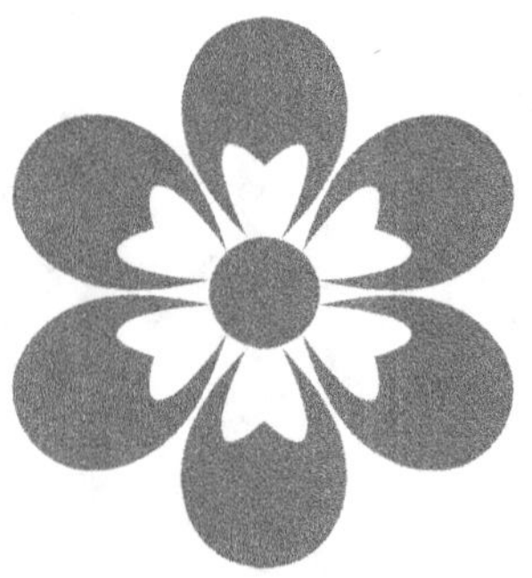

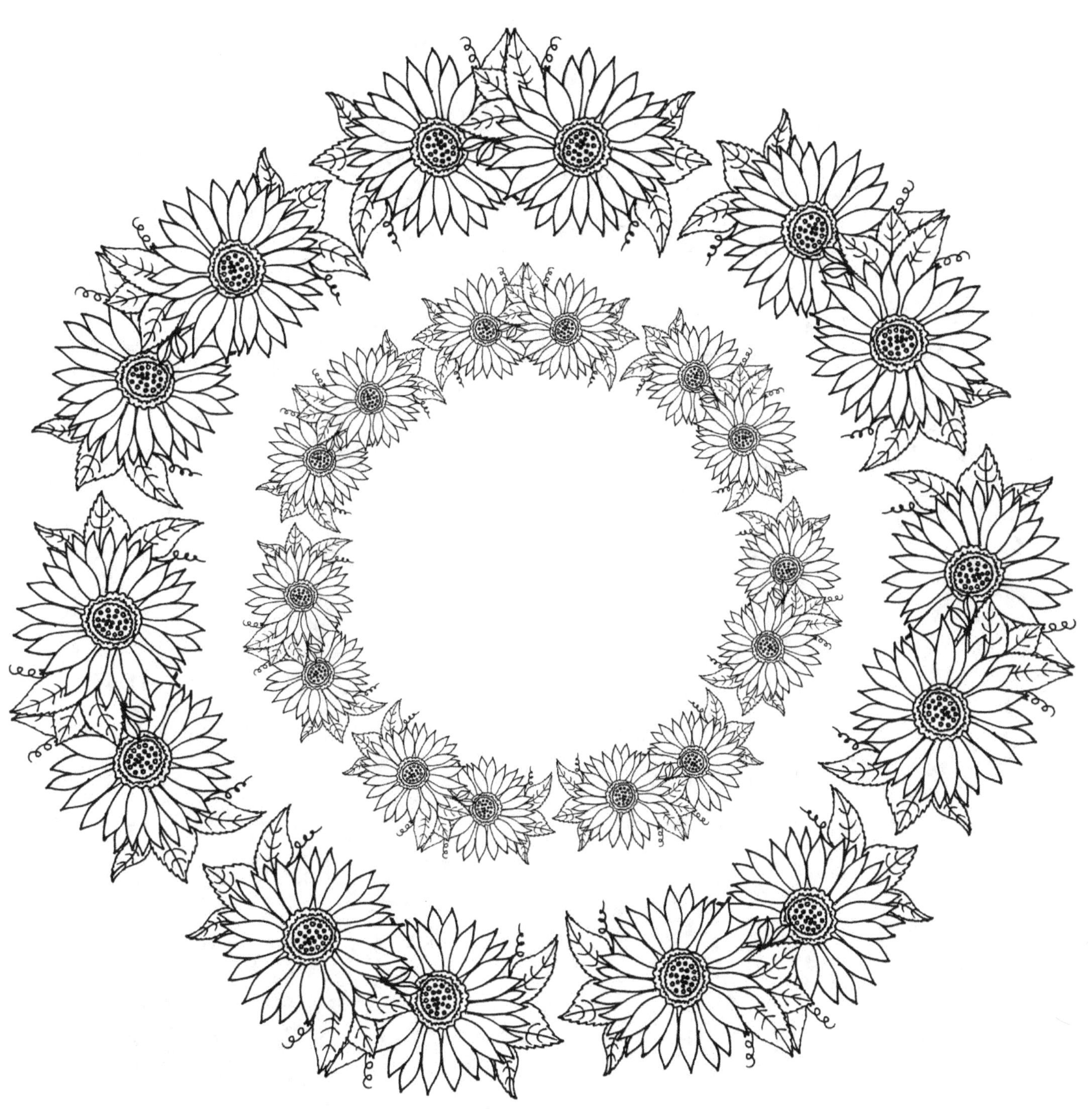

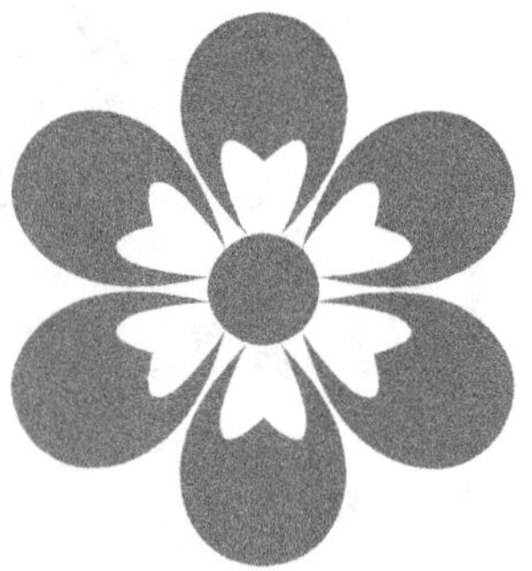

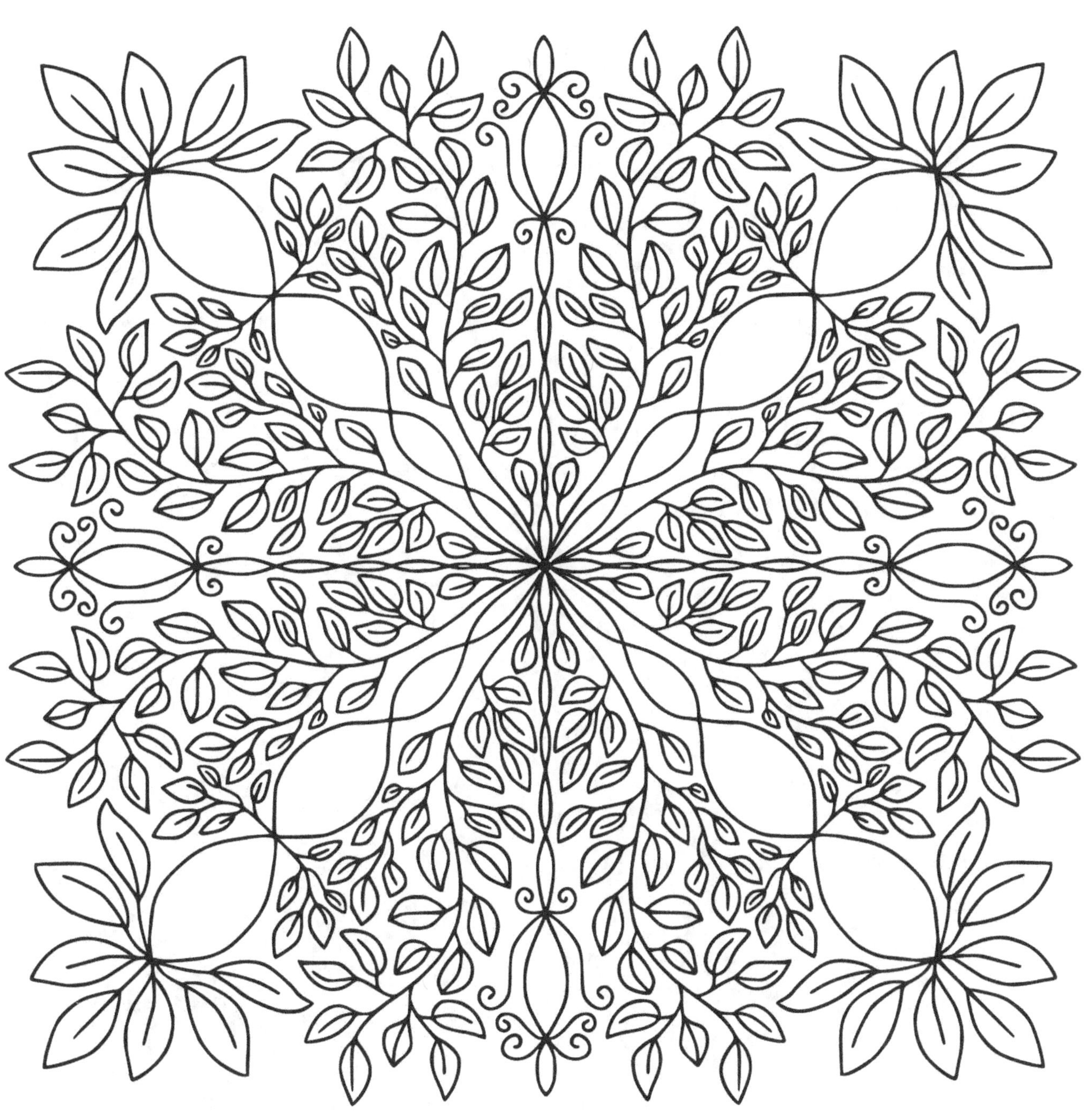

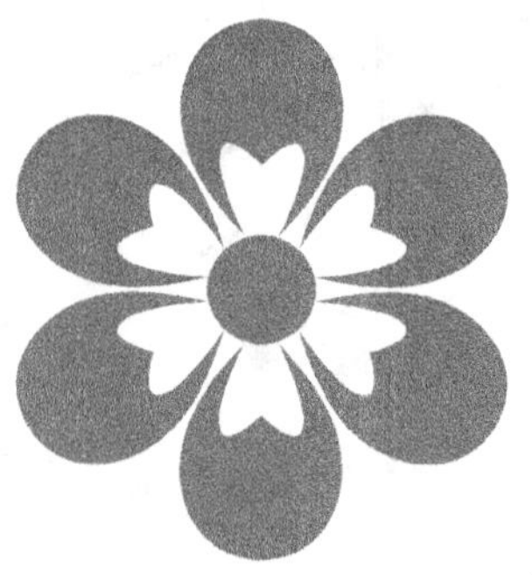

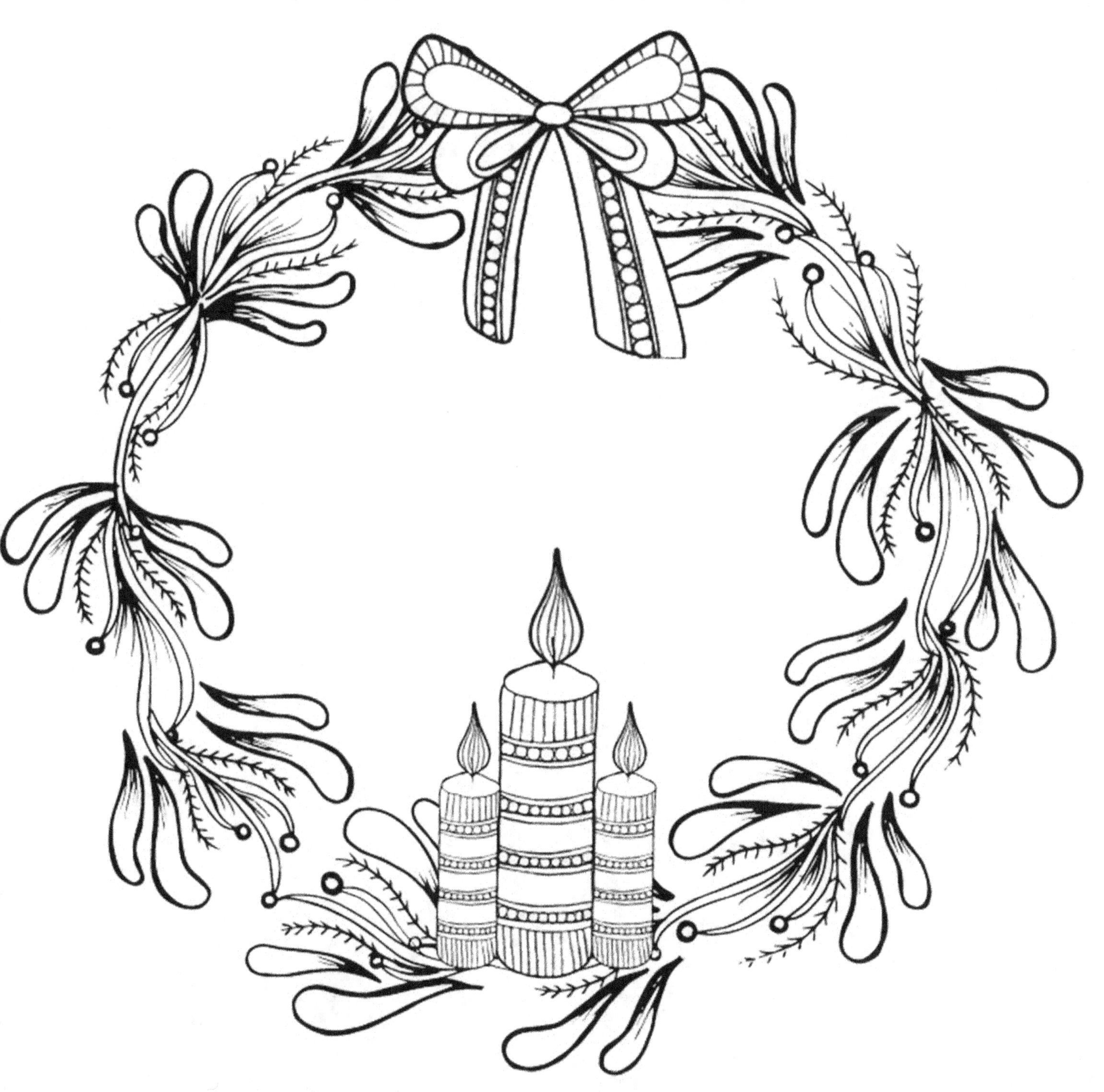

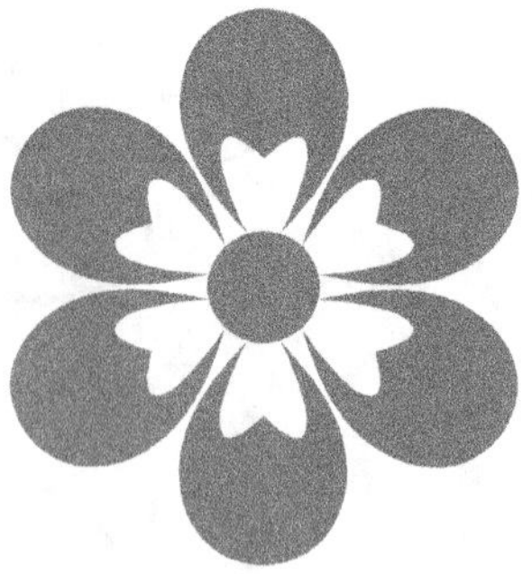

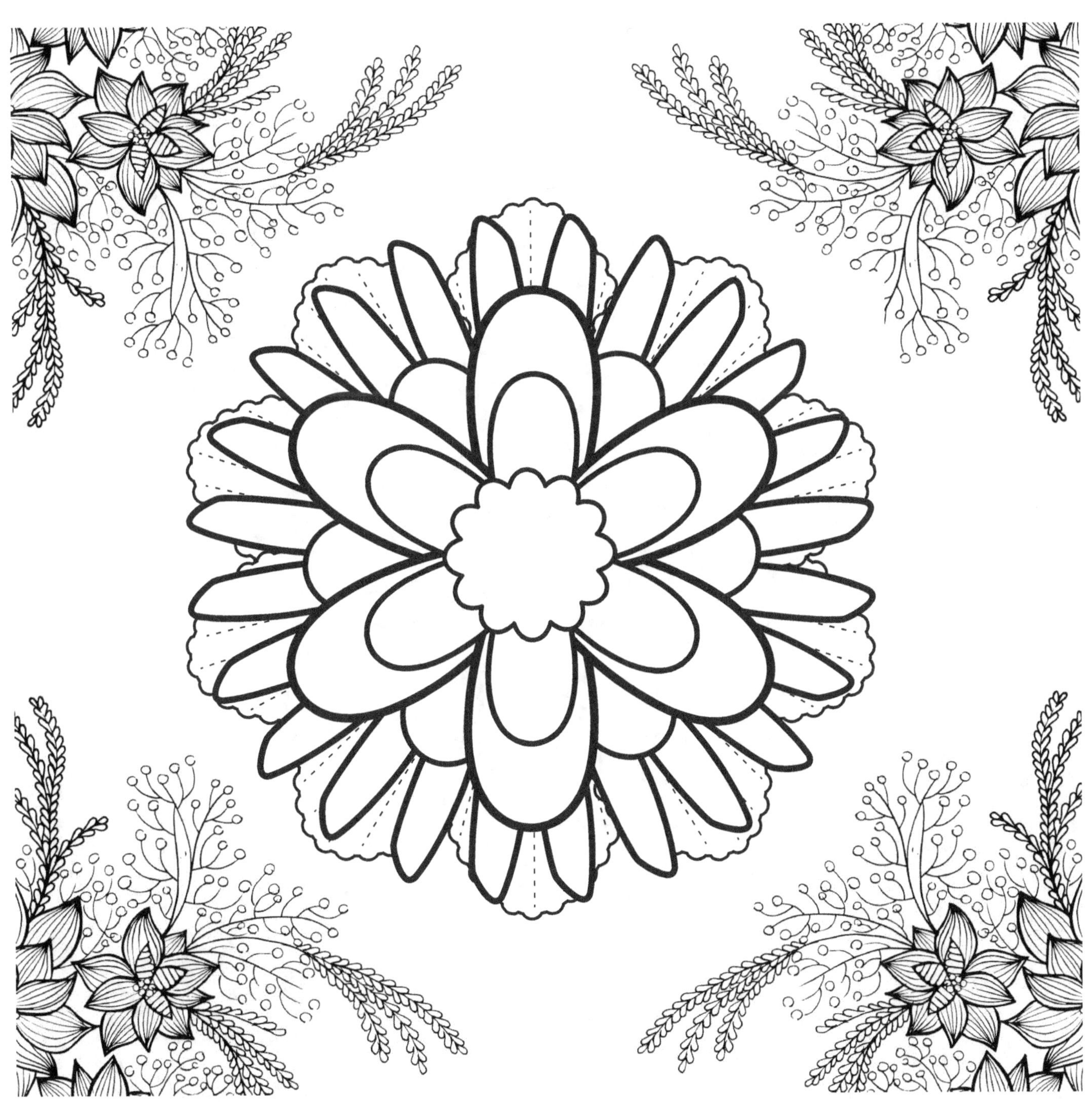

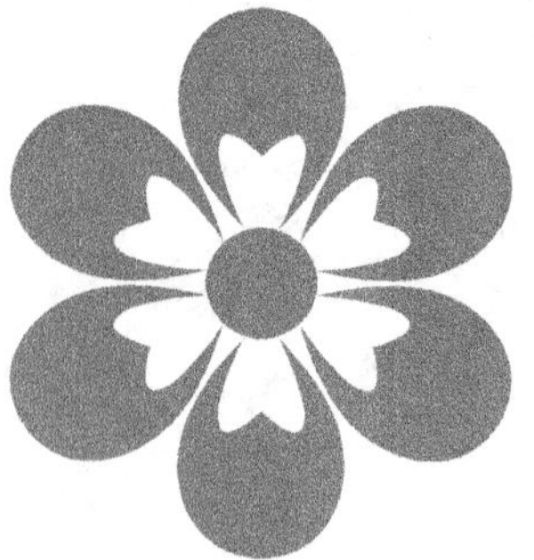

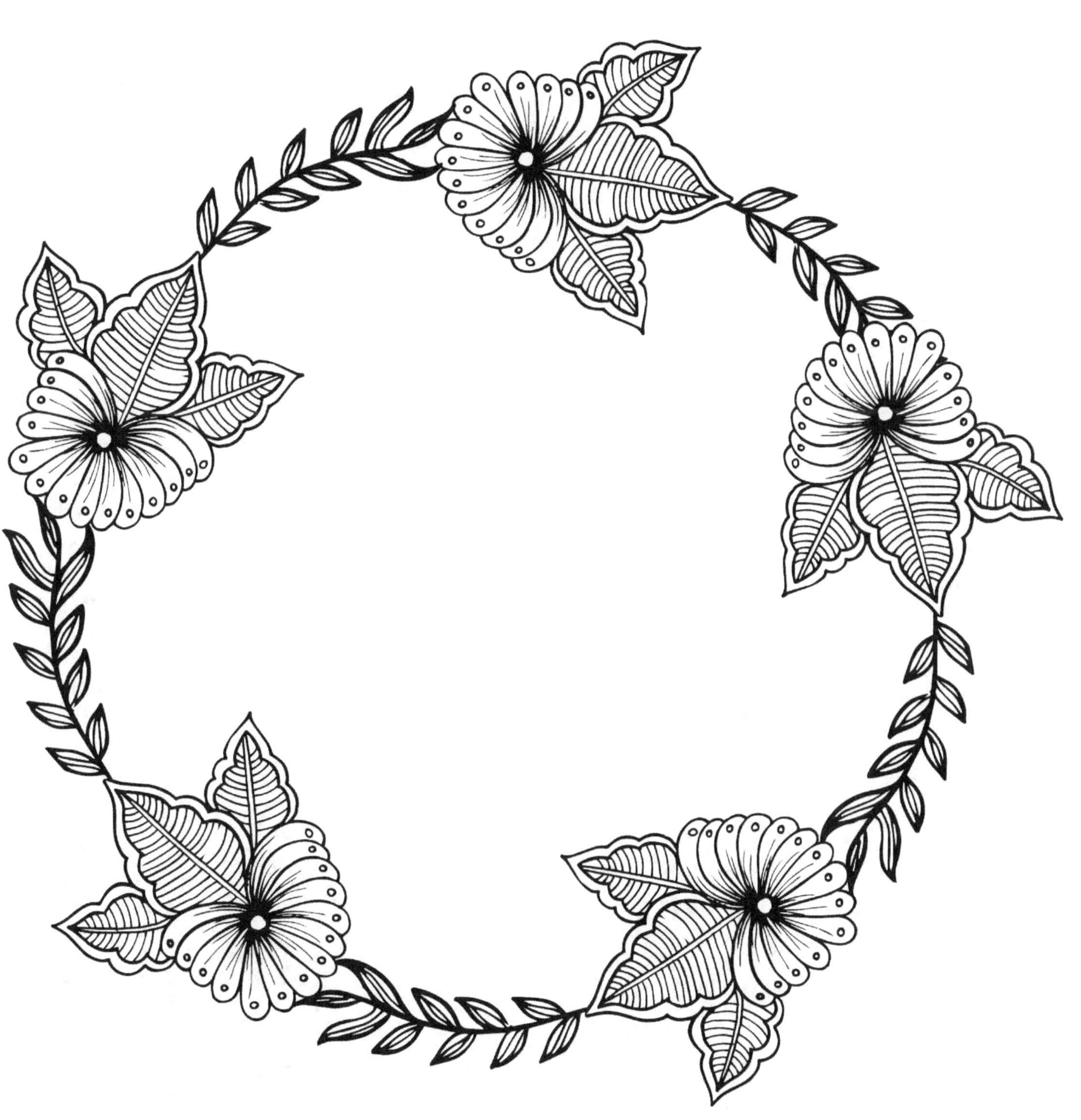

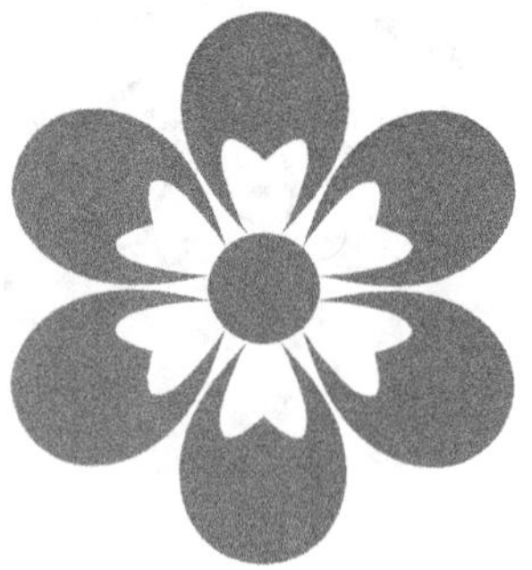

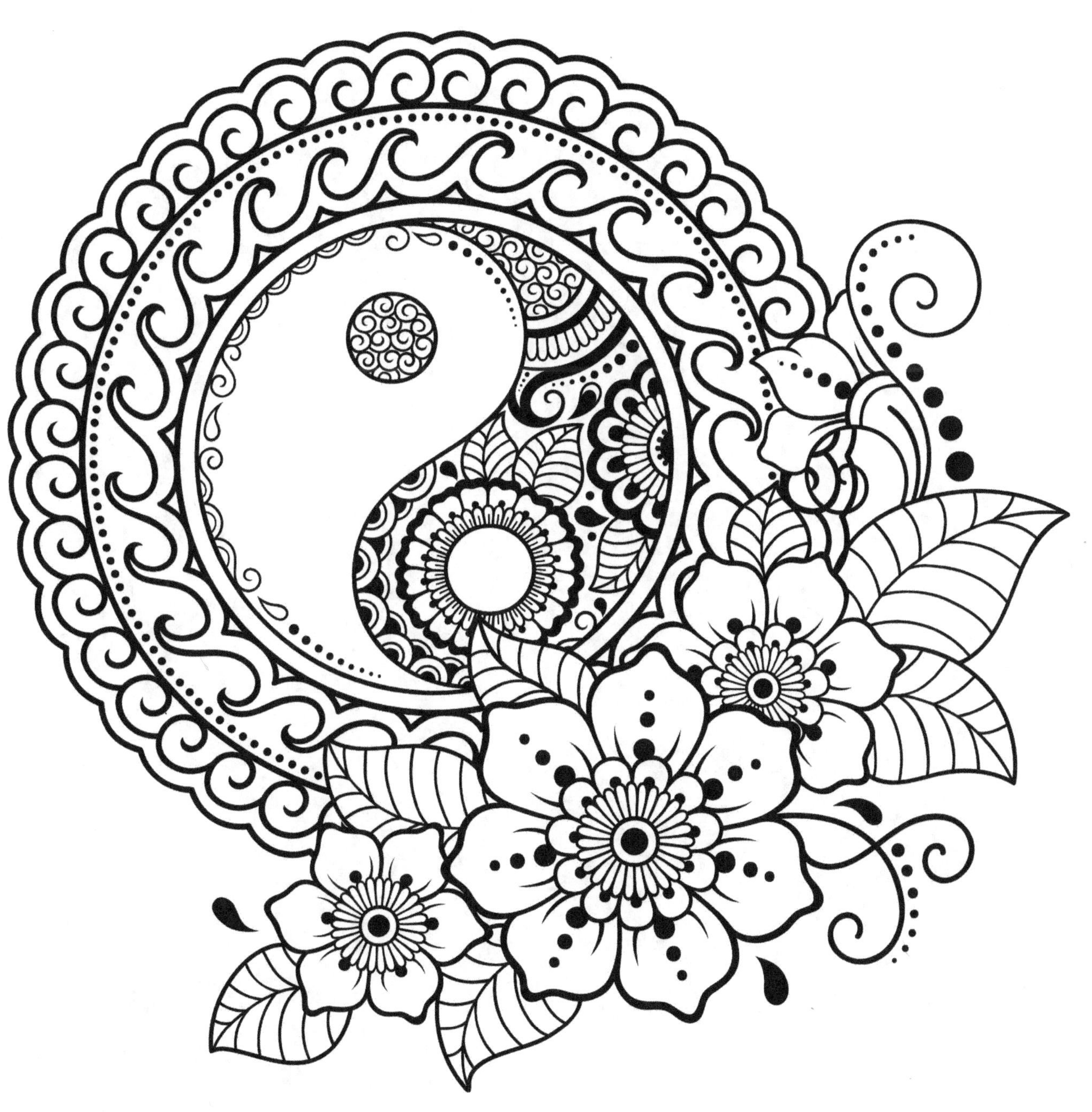

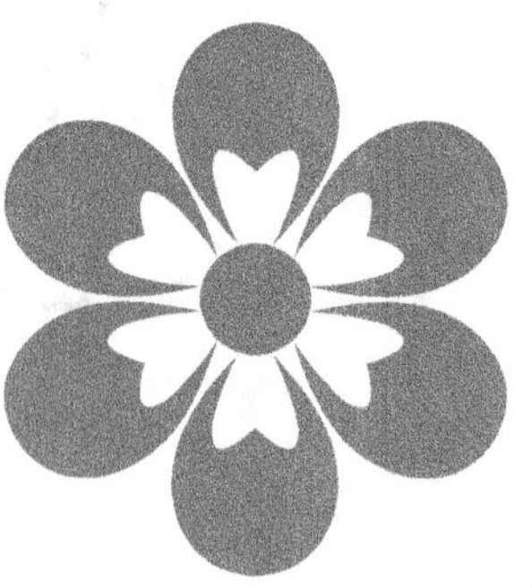

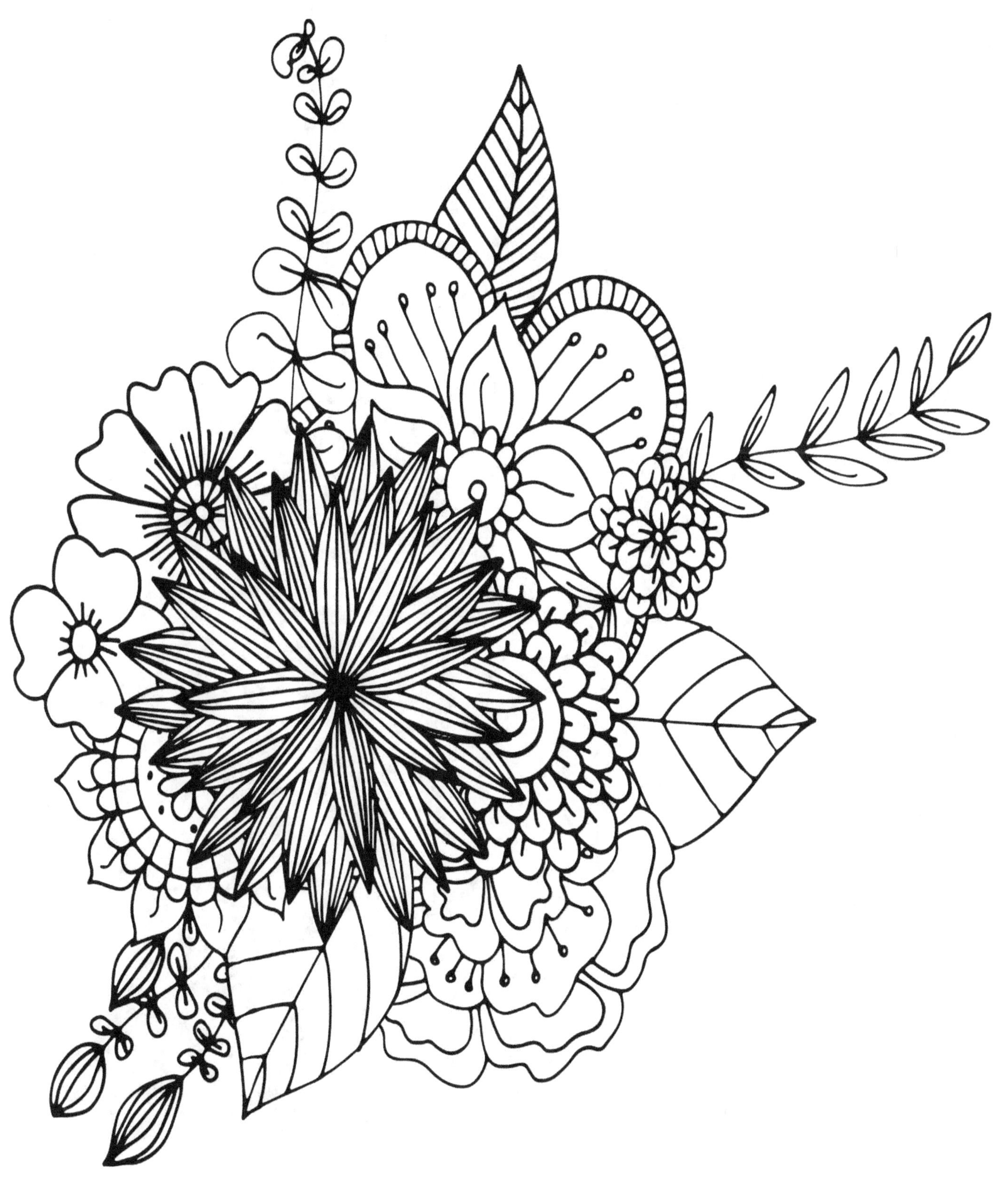

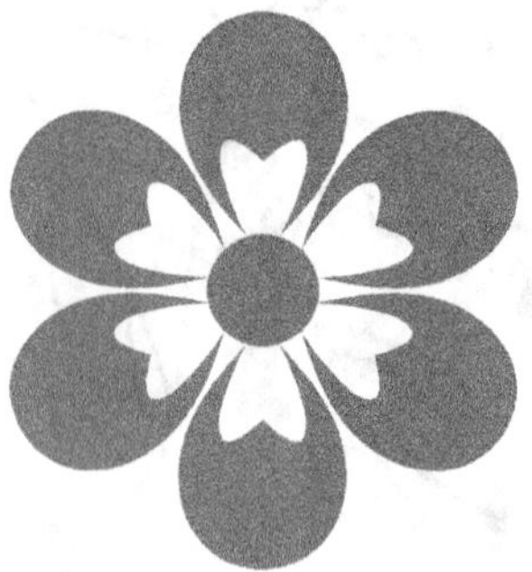

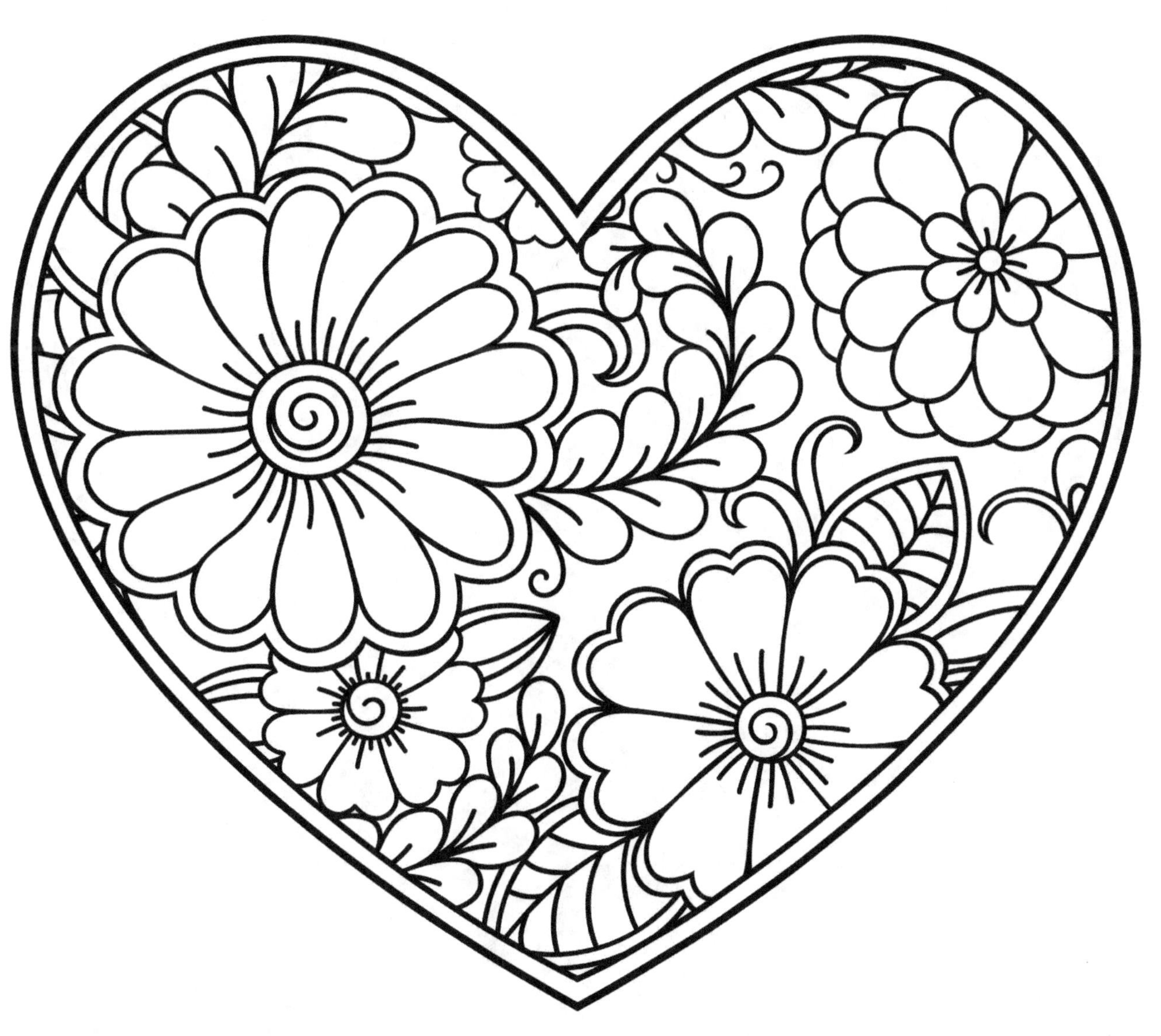

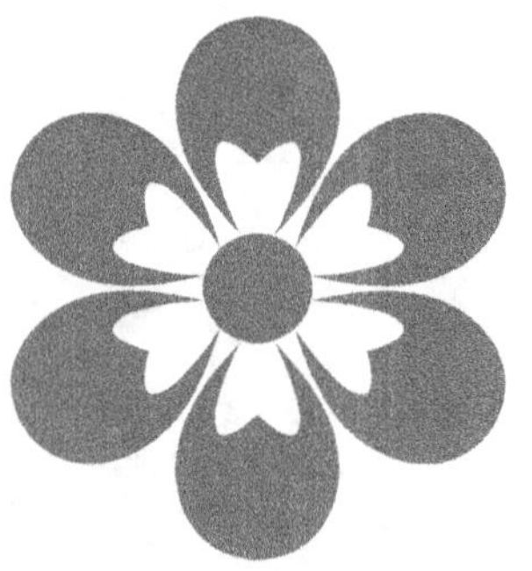

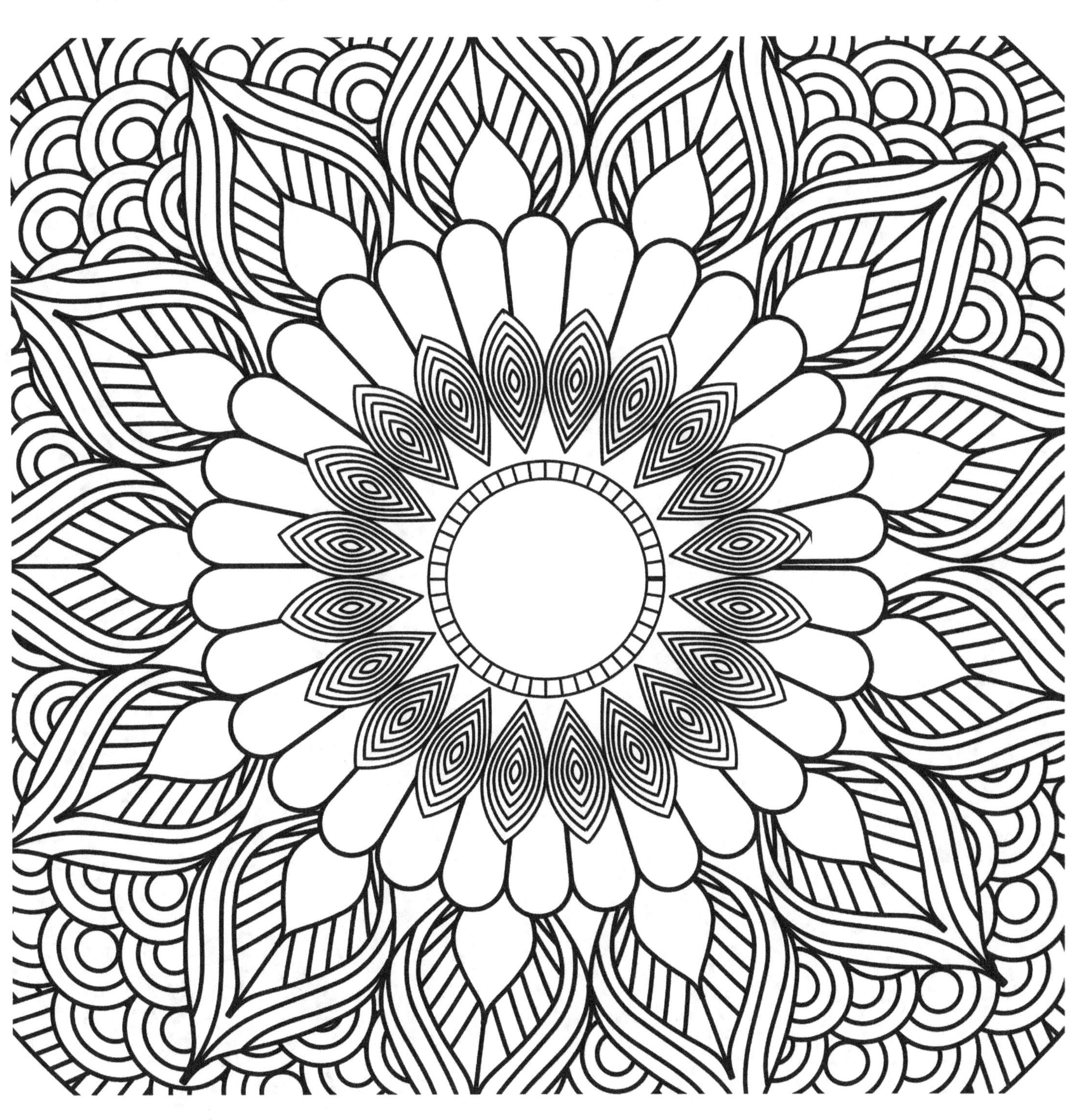

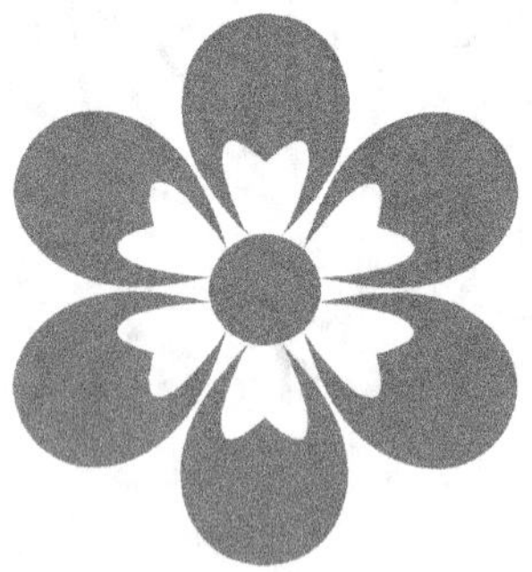

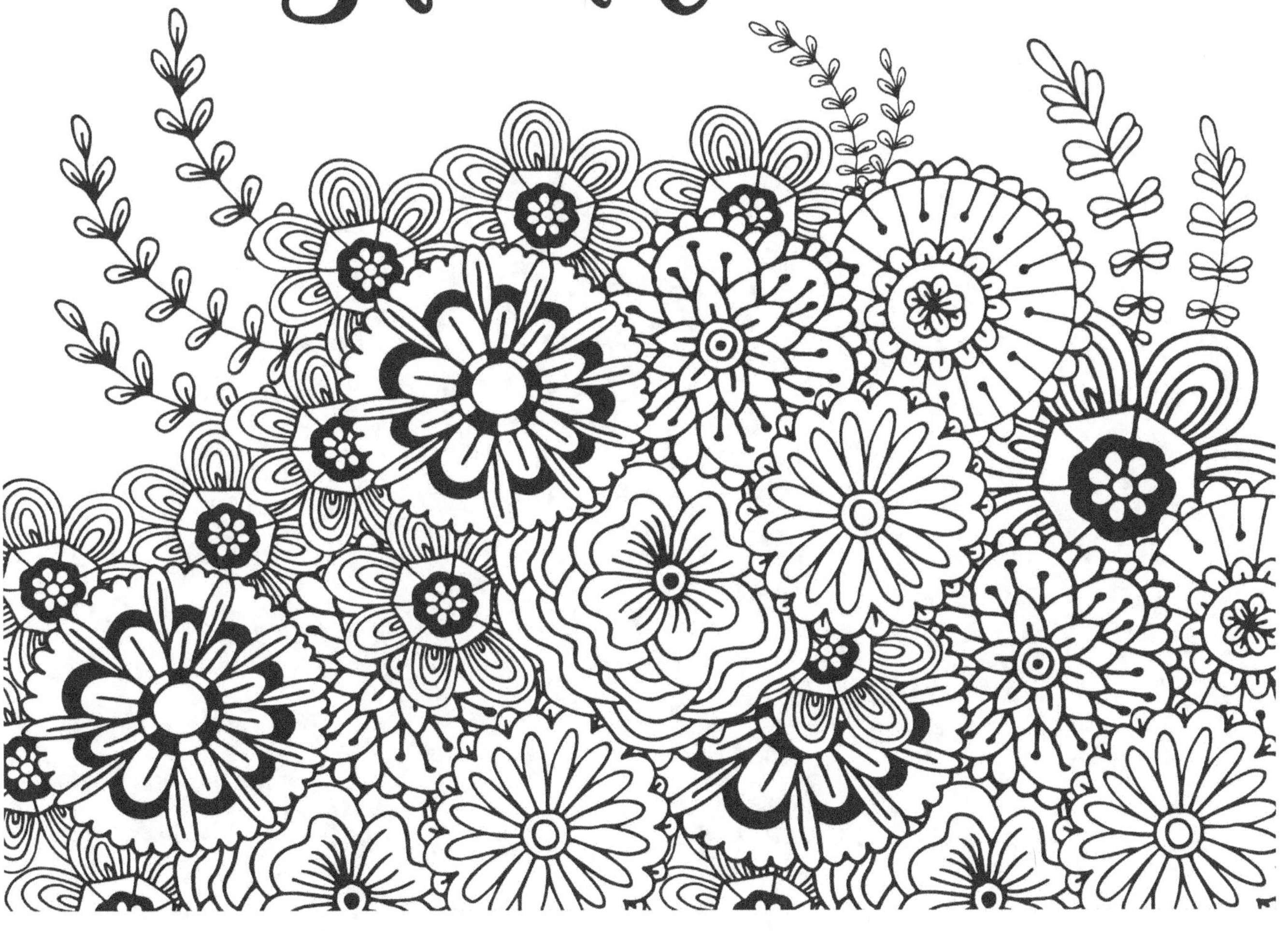

hello
Summer

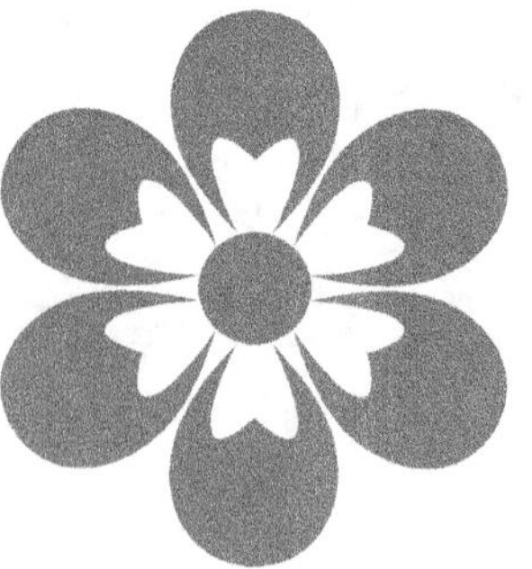

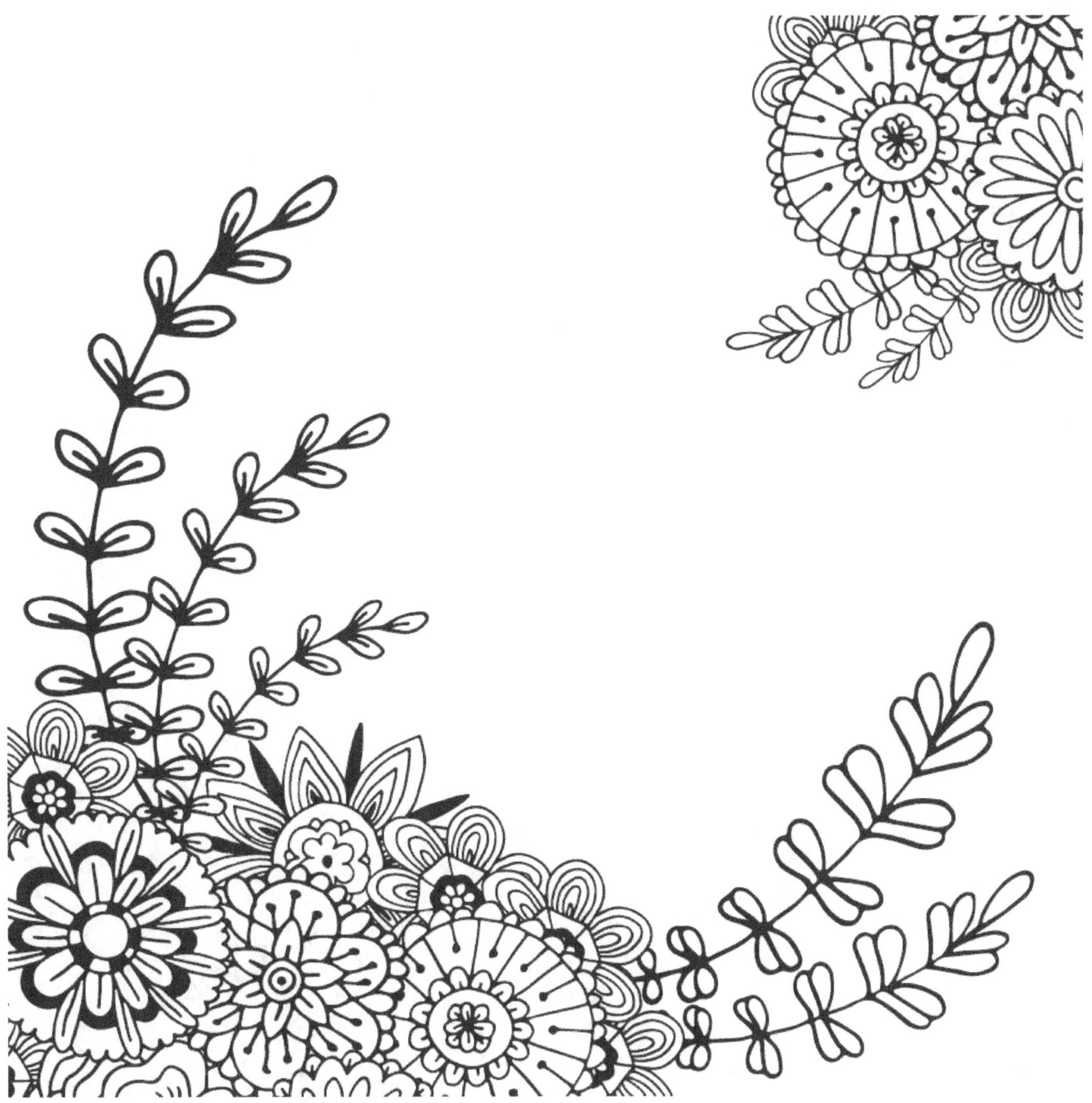

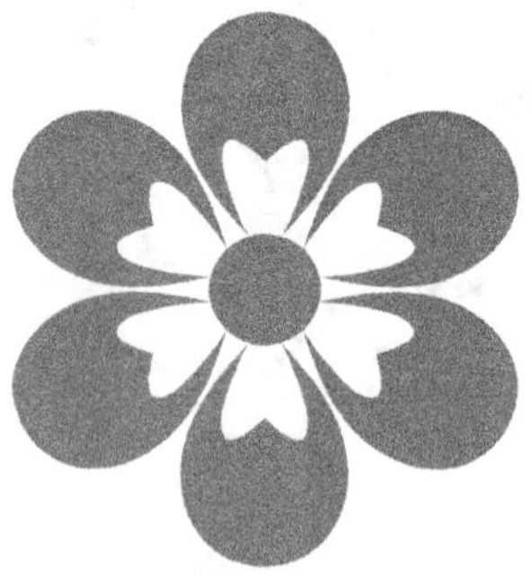

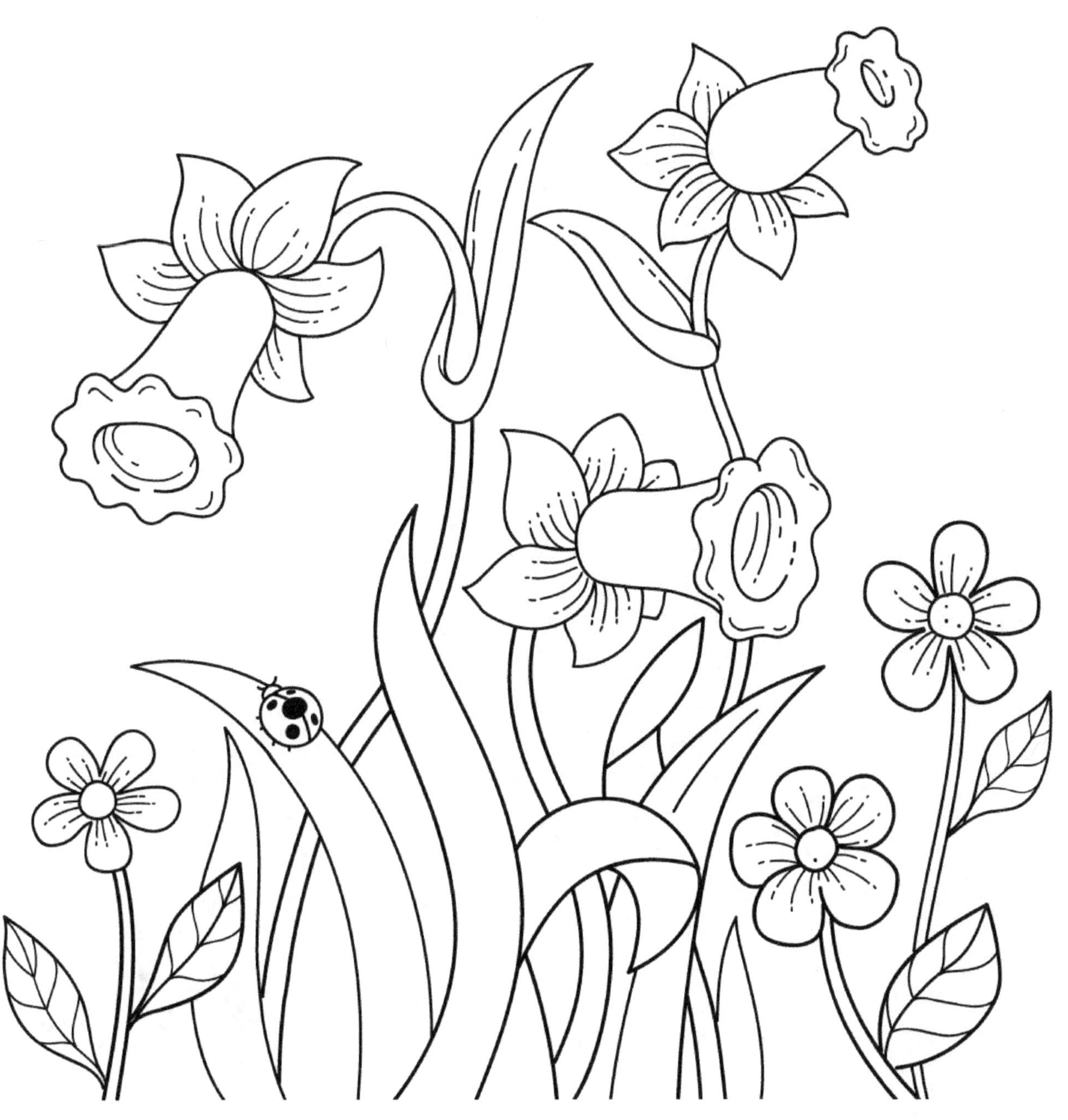

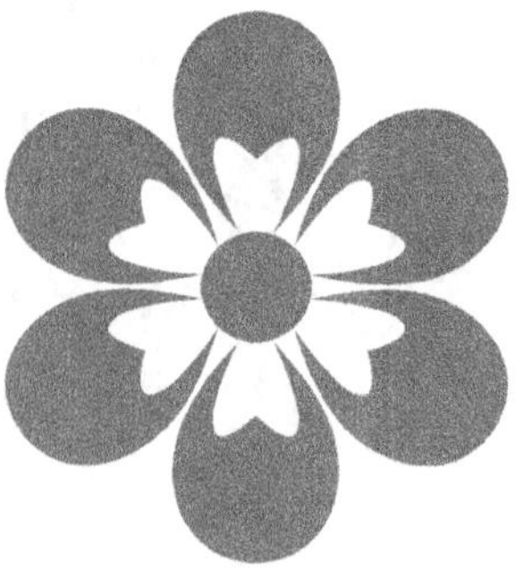

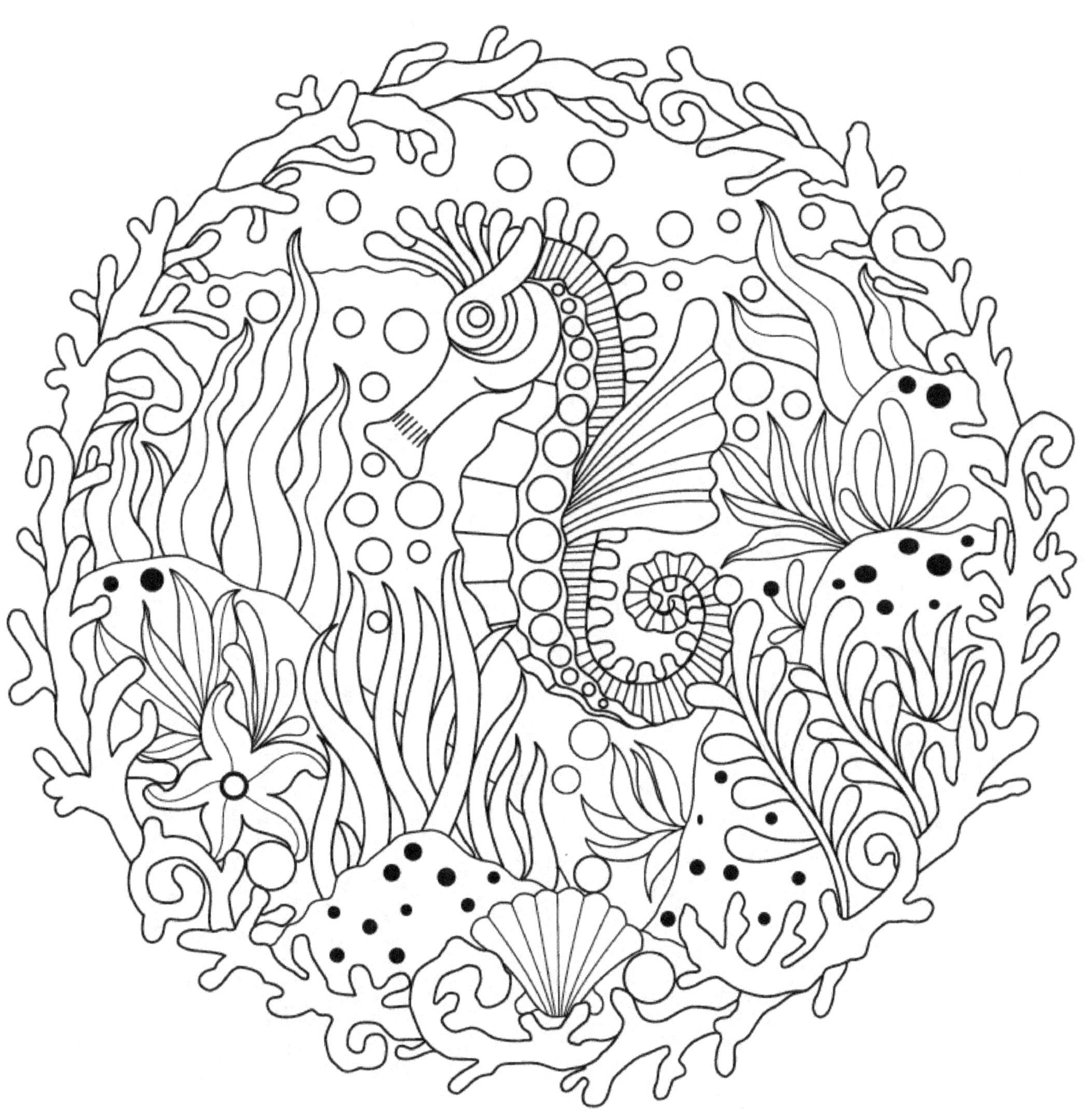

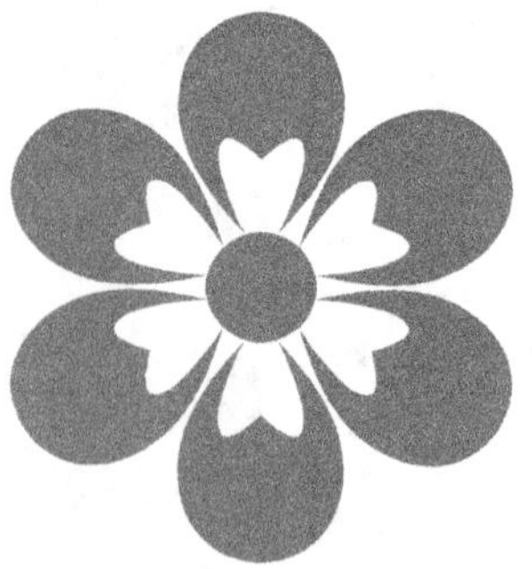

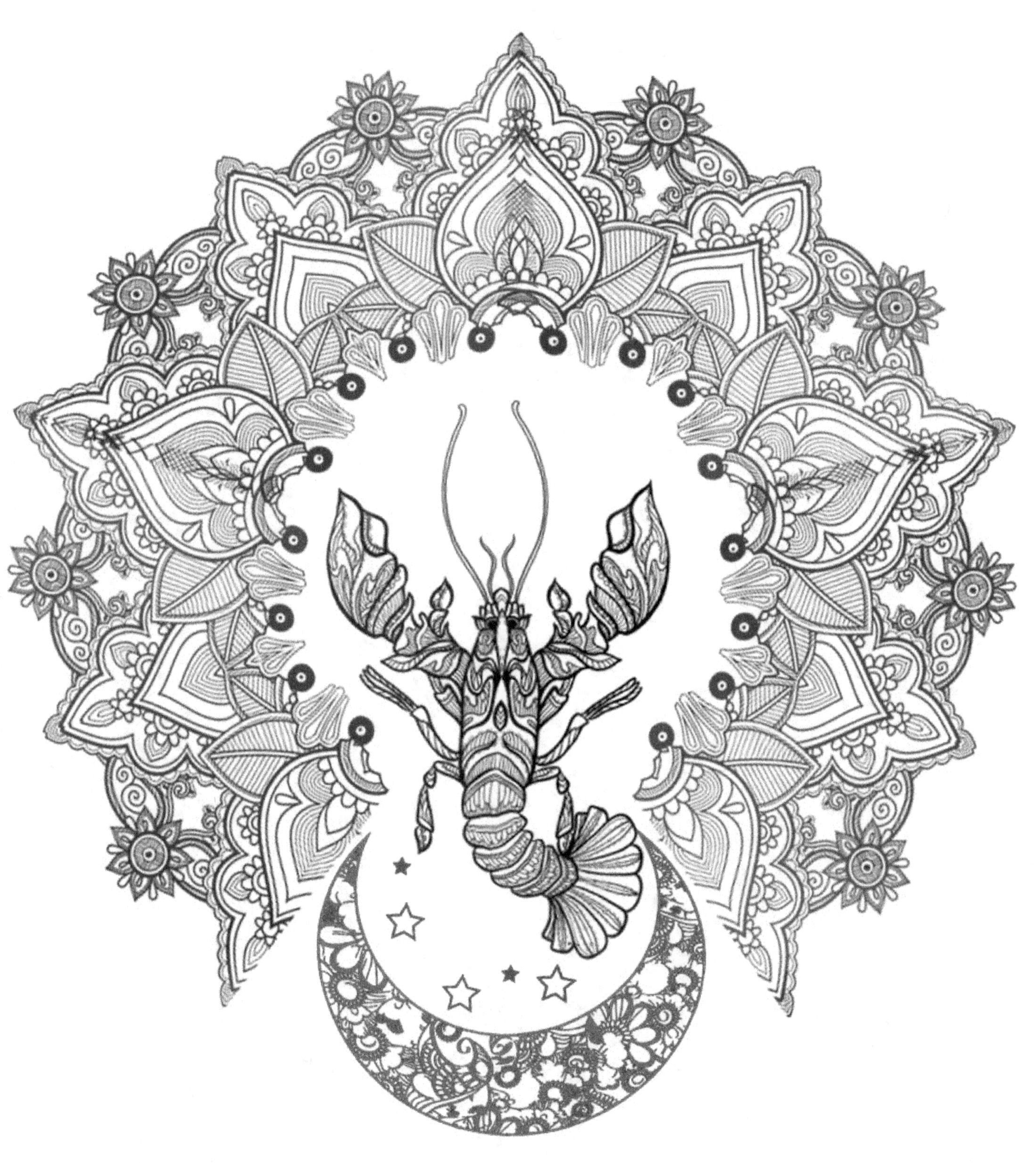

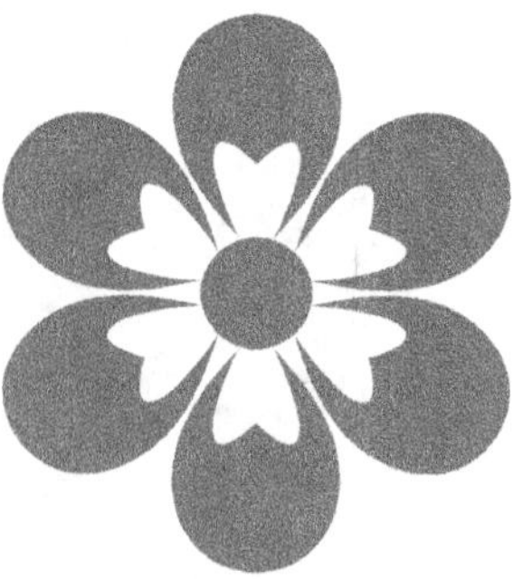

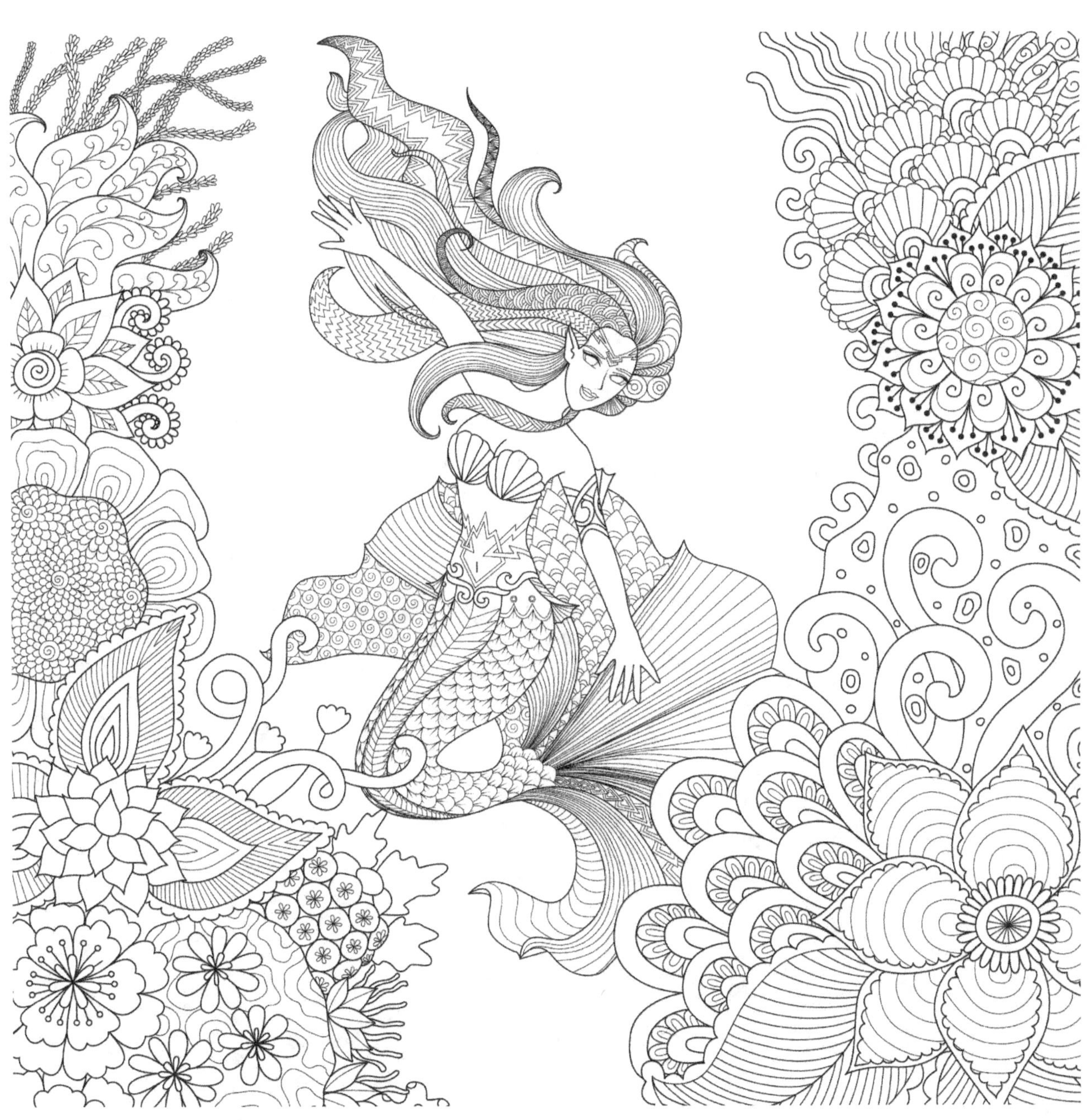

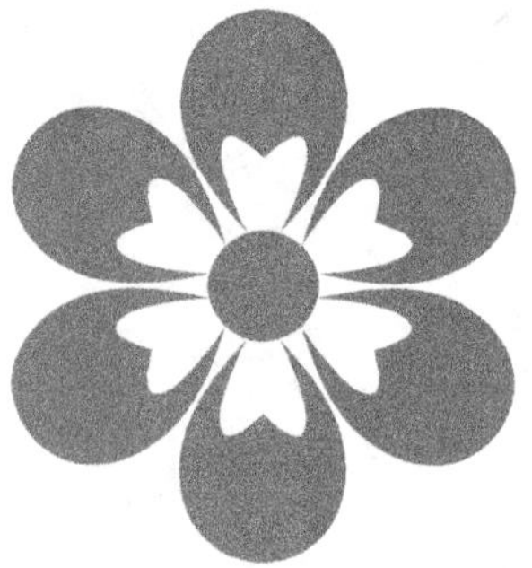

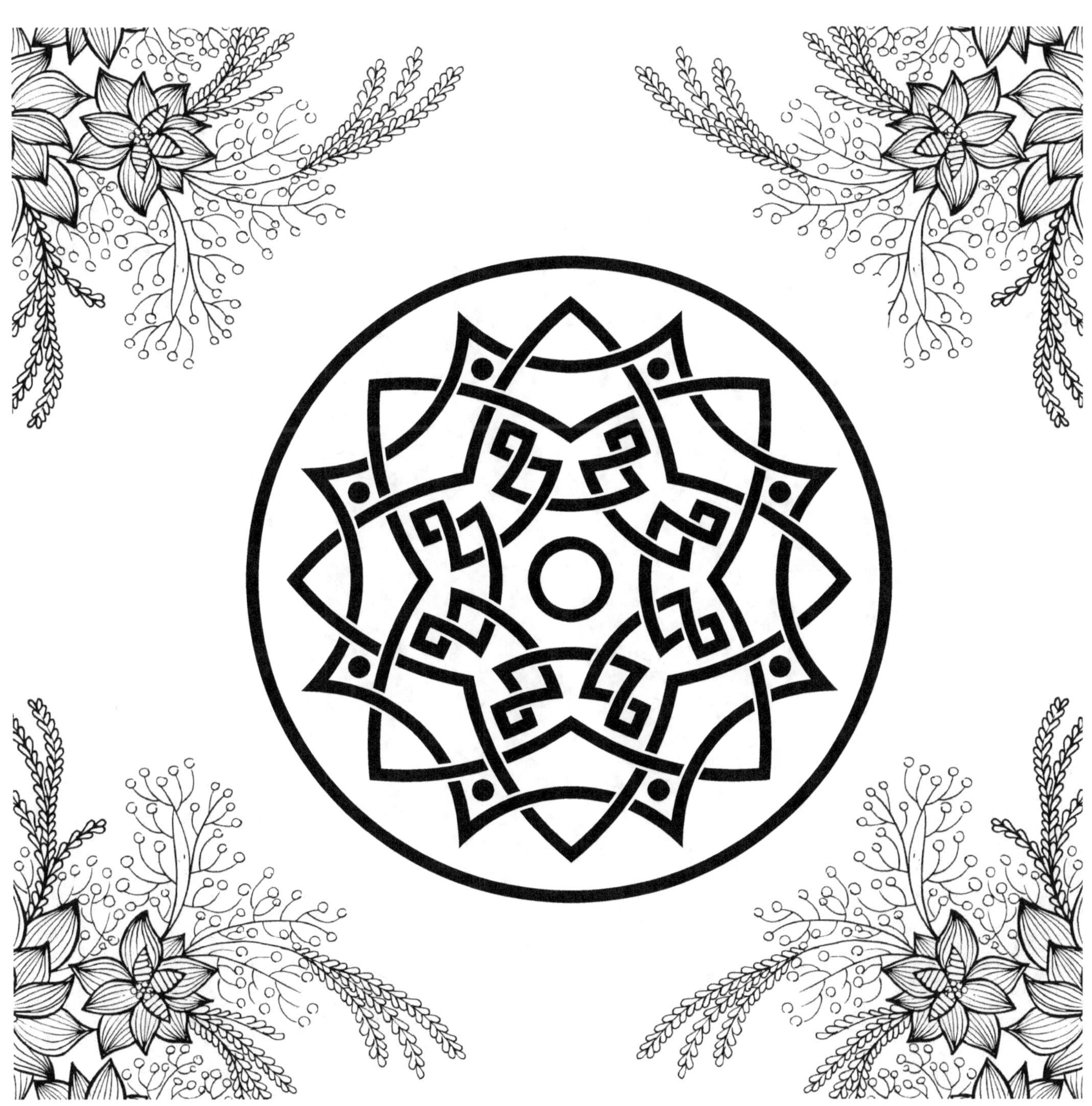

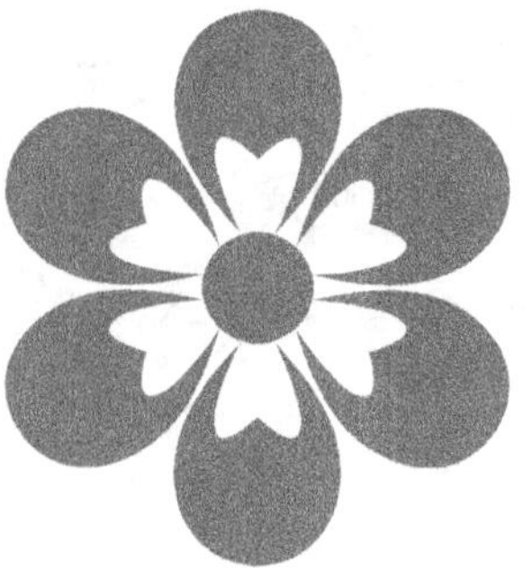

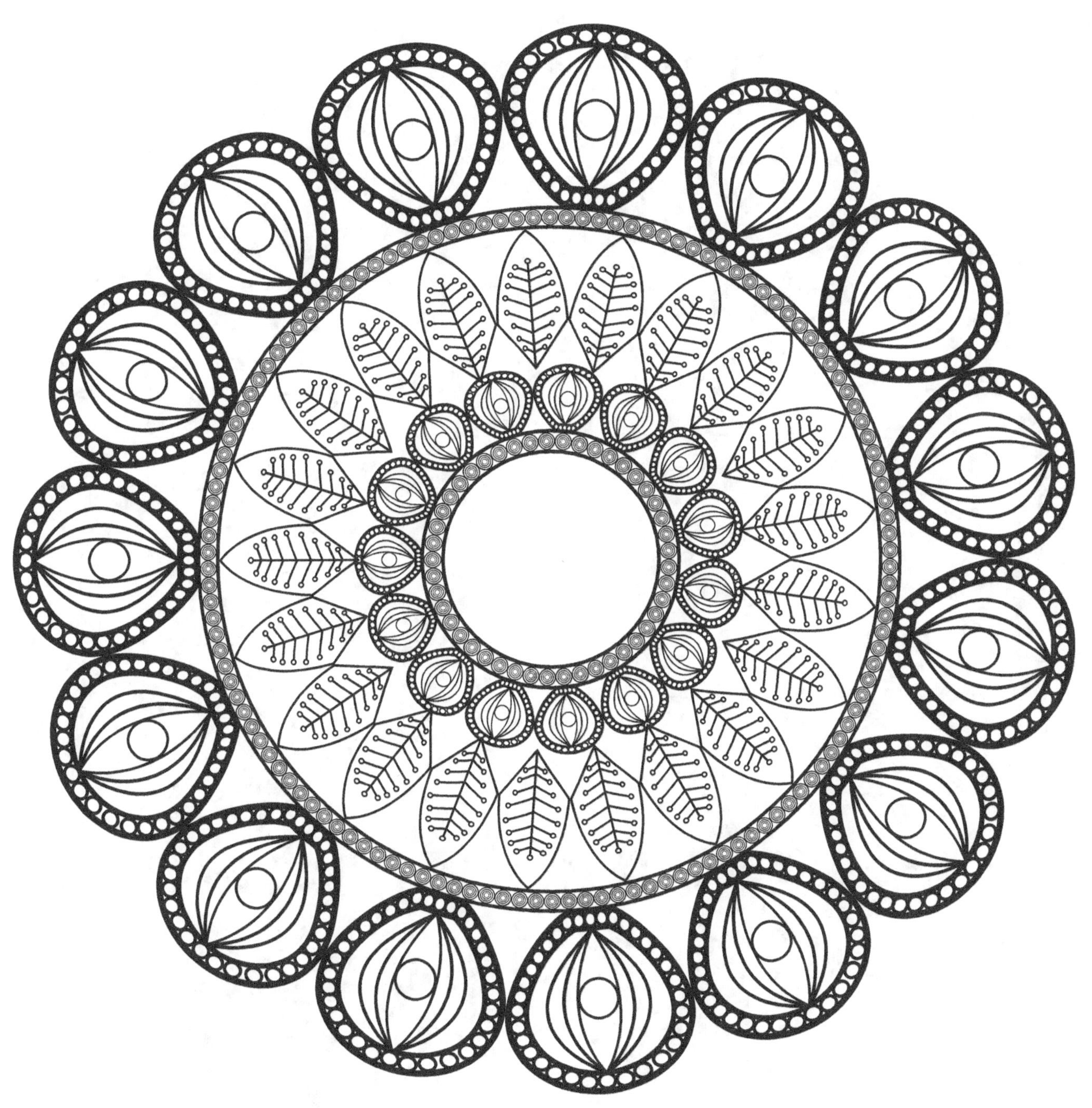

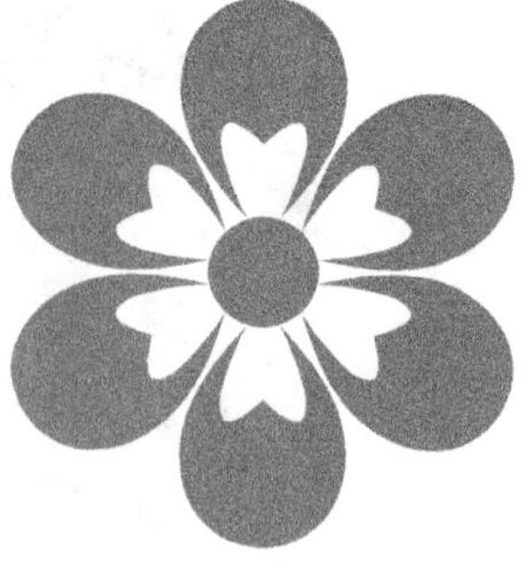

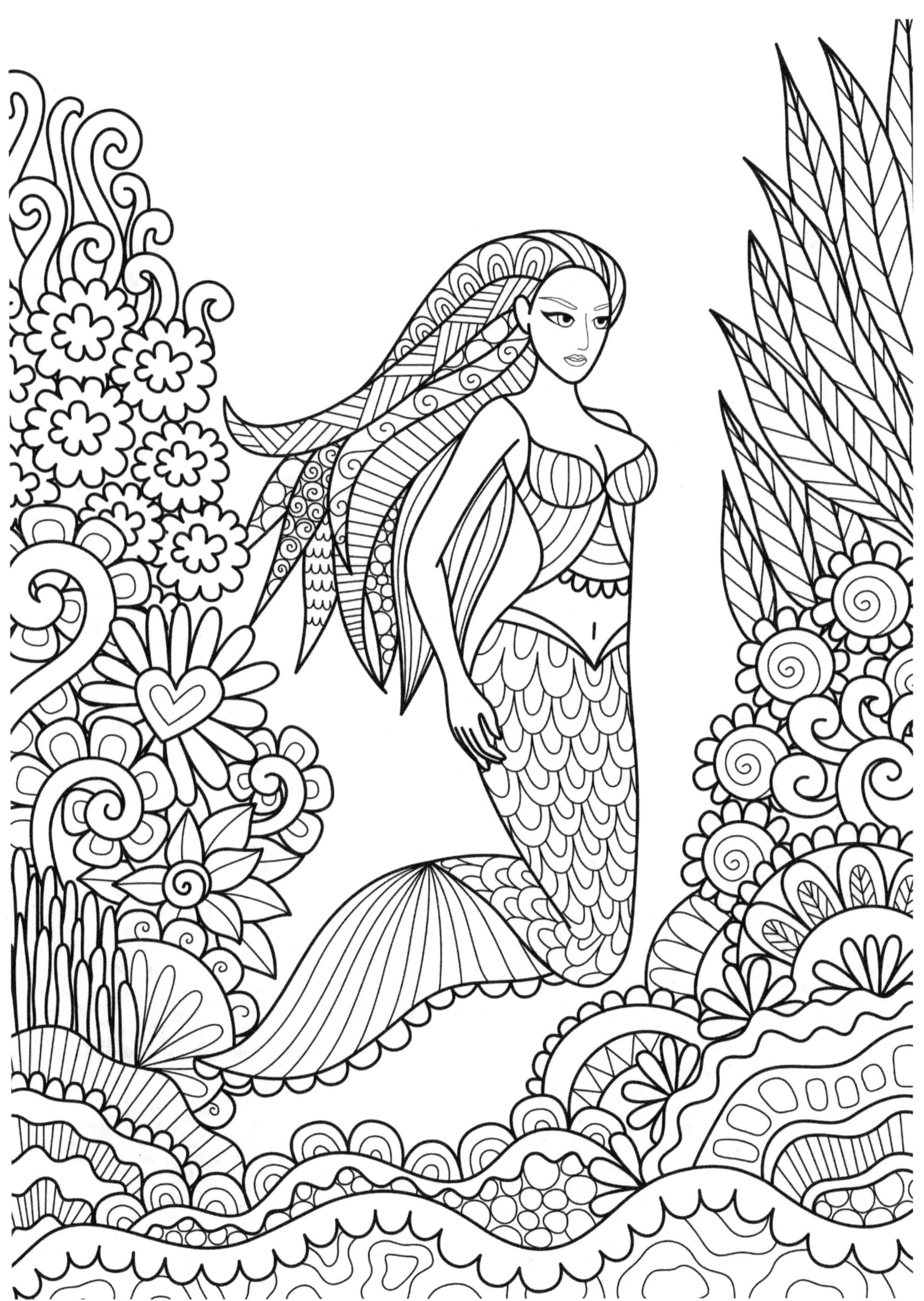

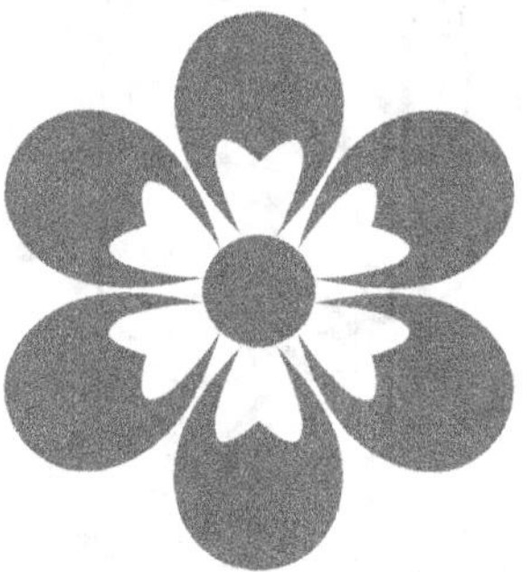

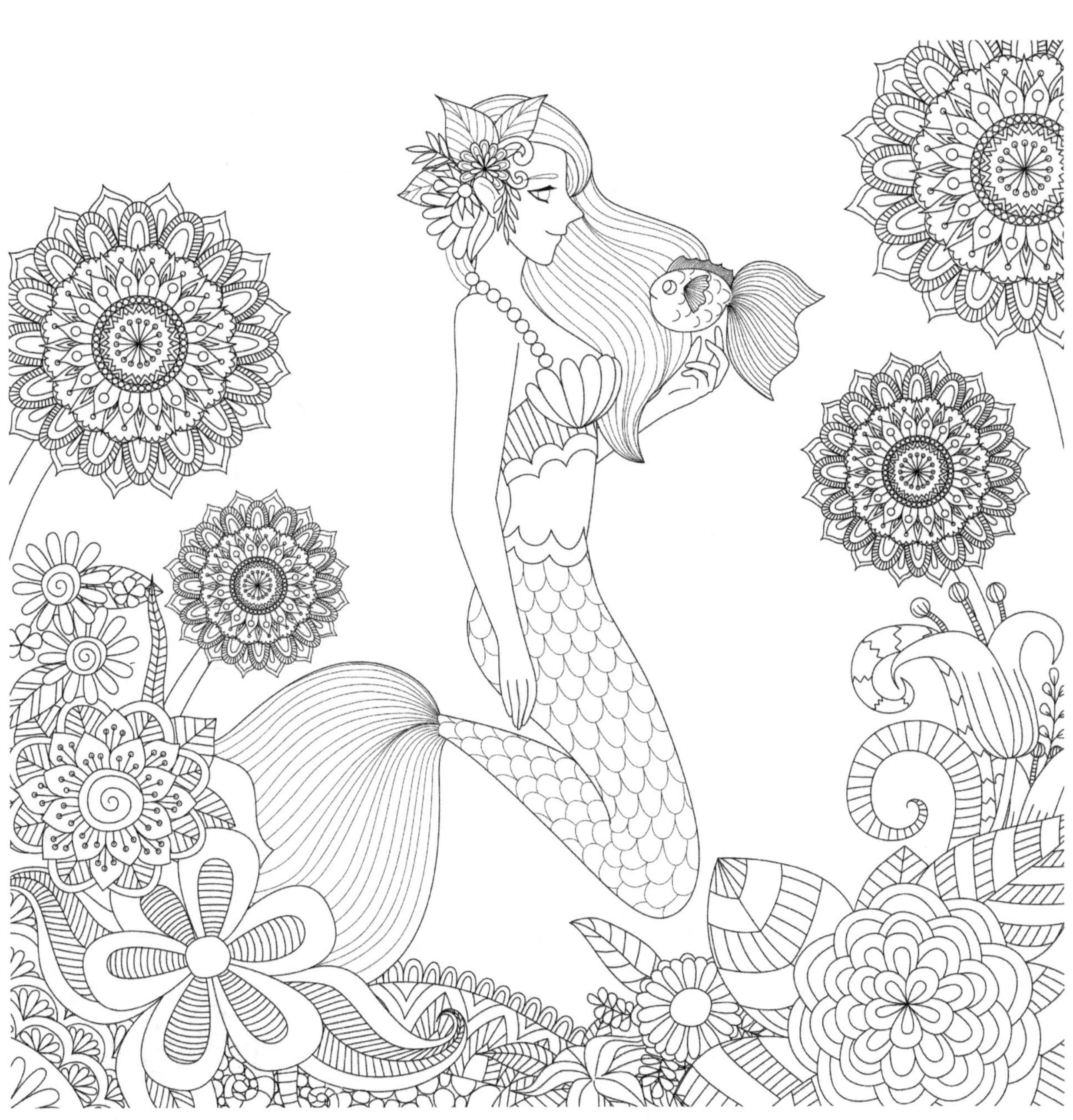

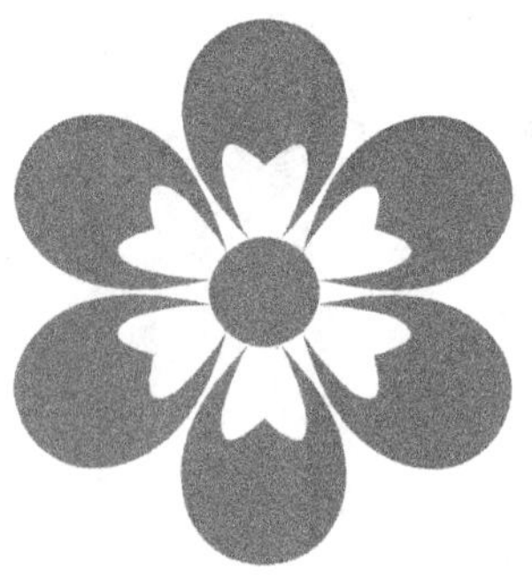

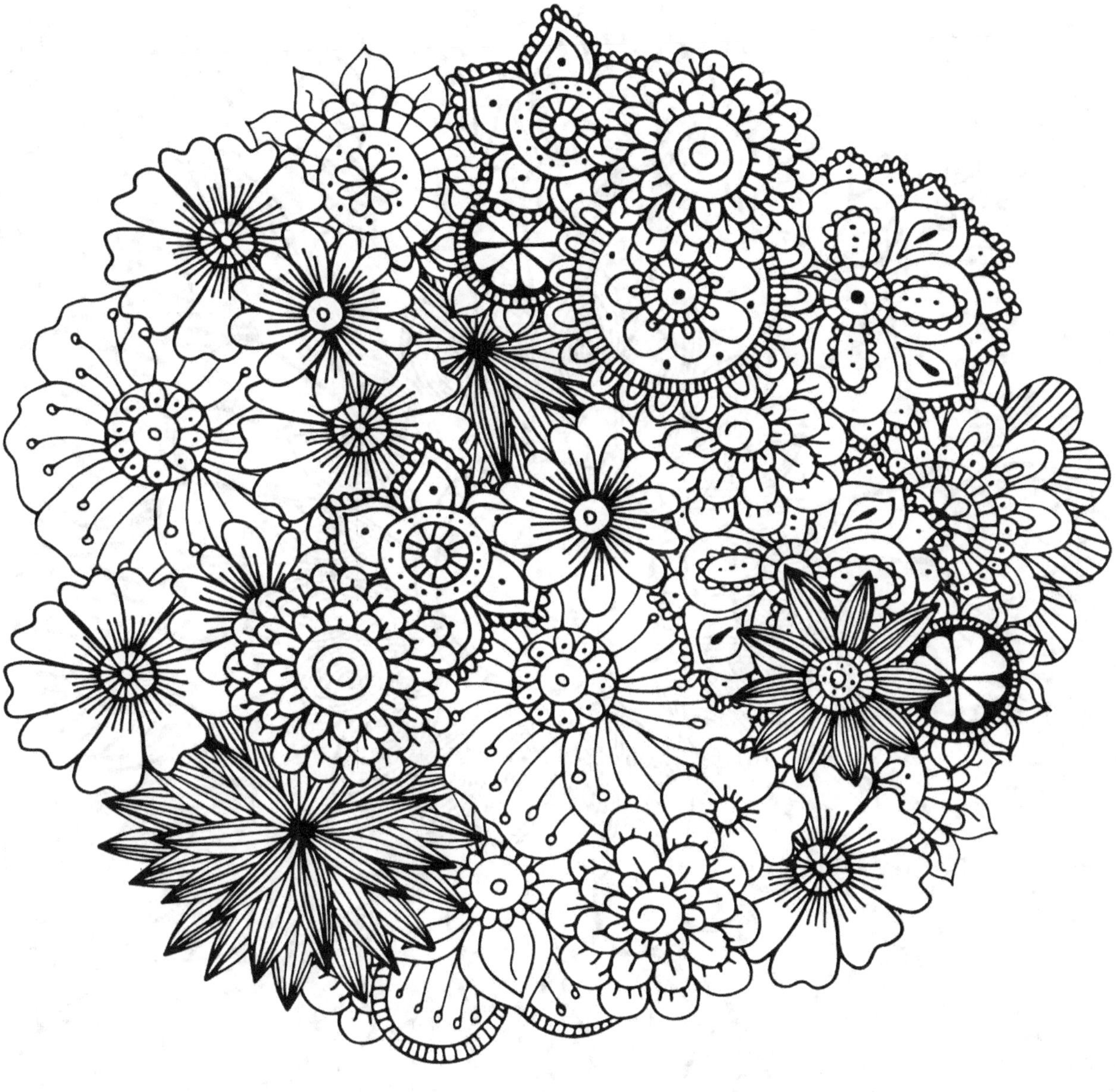

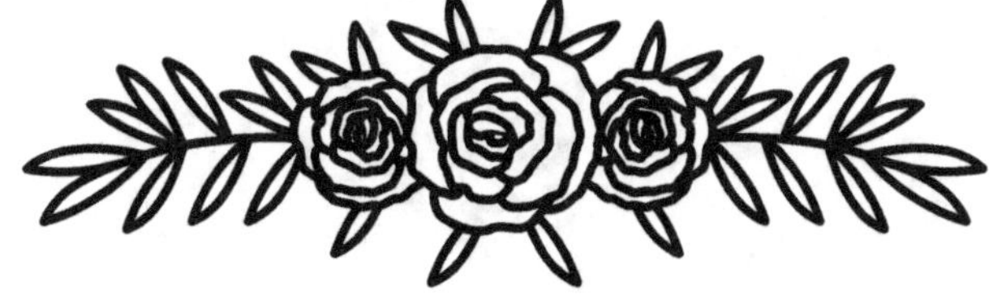

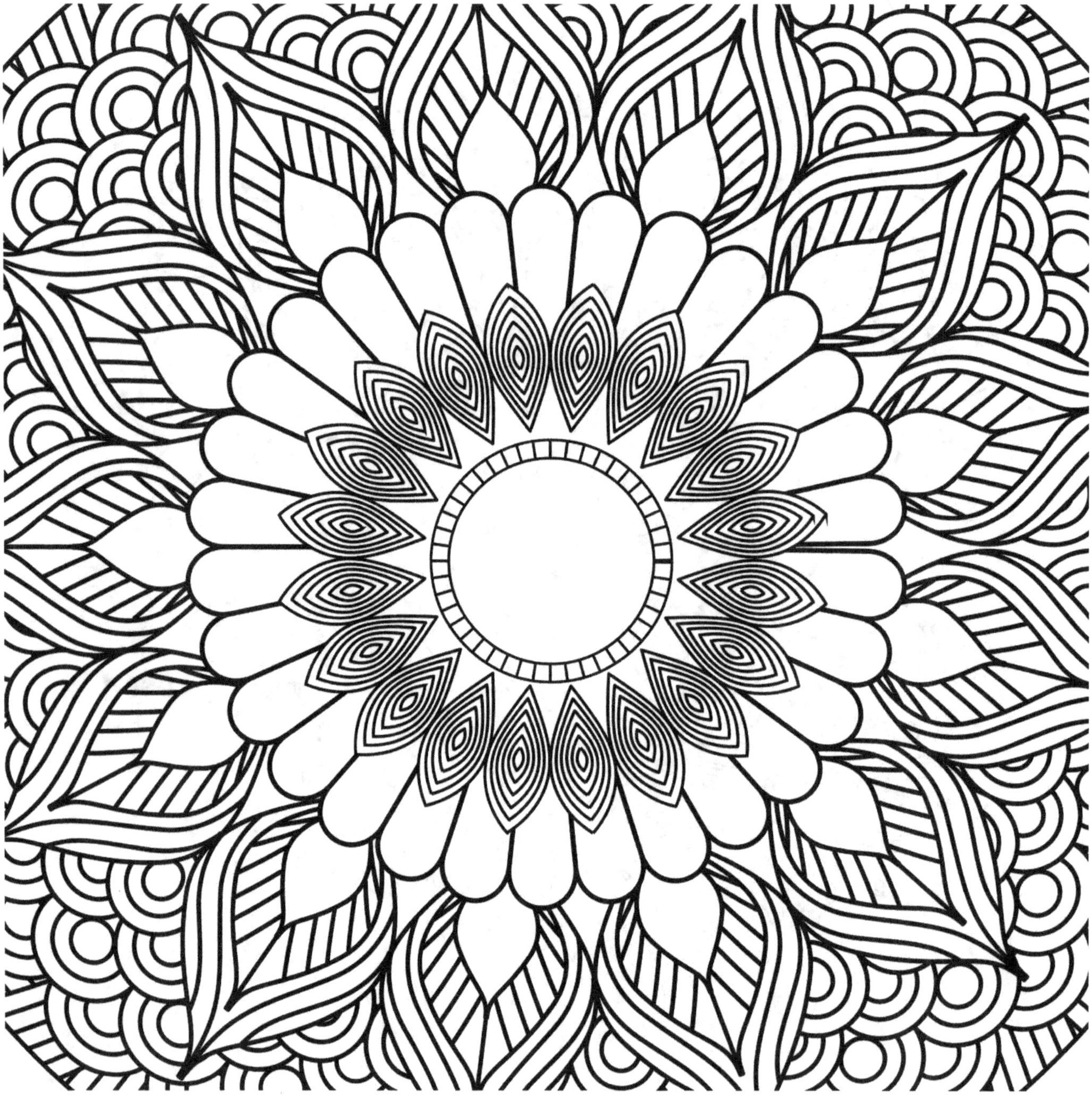

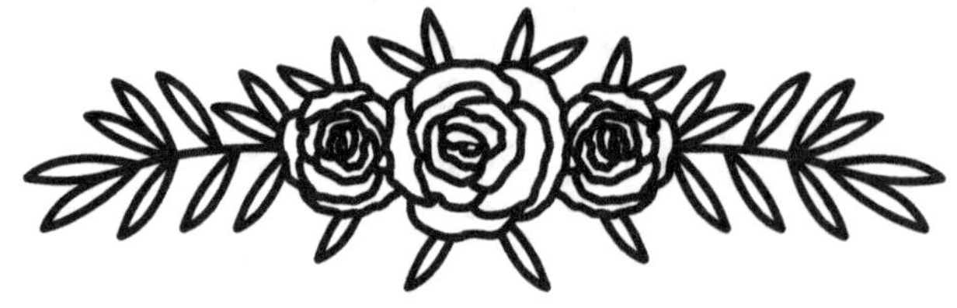

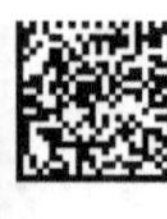